DIGITAL CLOCK

a collection of poems
in celebration of life

Elizabeth Lavers

DIGITAL CLOCK

a collection of poems
in celebration of life

Elizabeth Lavers

ISBN: 9780-9572053-2-1

Published by Easy Balance Books in conjunction with Writersworld, this book is produced entirely in the UK, is available to order from most book shops in the United Kingdom, and is also globally available via UK-based Internet book retailers and www.amazon.com.

Copy edited by Sue Croft

Cover photography & design by Martin Shute in collaboration with Jag Lall

www.writersworld.co.uk

WRITERSWORLD
2 Bear Close Flats
Bear Close
Woodstock
Oxfordshire
OX20 1JX
United Kingdom
☎ 01993 812500
☎ 0044 1993 812500

The text pages of this book are produced via an independent certification process that ensures the trees from which the paper is produced come from well managed sources that exclude the risk of using illegally logged timber while leaving options to use post-consumer recycled paper as well.

The author

Having previously been resident in France, Holland, Libya, Oman, Nigeria and Venezuela, Elizabeth Lavers now lives in London and Sussex, but continues to travel extensively. Her work has appeared in the Anglican Theological Review, and in 2014 her book of New Testament-based poems (' . . . *and there was Light'*, ISBN 978-0-9572053-0-7) was published by Easy Balance Books in conjunction with Writersworld. This book is used in churches of different denominations as a source of readings and seasonal plays for voices.

The author is the Club Poet of the Royal Thames Yacht Club, the oldest continuously active yacht club in existence, founded in 1775. Included in *Digital Clock* are two poems she was recently commissioned to write for ceremonies marking the centenary of the Gallipoli landings. She is fluent in several languages and some of her translations into English verse appear in the book.

Engaging, light-hearted and witty, the poems in this book vary in tone and pace, reflecting an upbeat view of life, and cover a wide spectrum of themes from bird-watching to taxi drivers and postmen, changing seasons, faraway places and quiet moments. All the poems are intended to be read aloud.

The Poems

DIGITAL CLOCK :

HOME OR AWAY :

DANDELION SUN :

VOYAGE OF DISCOVERY :

IN OTHER WORDS - *poems translated by the author* :

DIGITAL CLOCK

CARELESS BOUNTY

Those far off days of summer heaven,
Villages with watermills,
Outings in the Austin Seven,
Sunshine on the Surrey Hills.

Daylong trips to greener places,
Expeditions to the sea;
Sunburned necks and arms and faces,
Scones and jam or fish for tea.

Apple cores, once thrown by cousins
Into hedges or the grass,
Grown to trees, still fruit in dozens
To delight us as we pass.

Apple trees by winding roads
Past Dorking, Guildford, Leatherhead,
Are bending, spilling juicy loads
Of yellow, golden-green and red.

Varieties considered lost
May still be glimpsed from car or train,
Out of reach, where they were tossed,
But shining in the autumn rain.

CORNUCOPIA

Rich harvests are ripening in the hedges
By Heckfield, Mattingley, Rotherwick,
Where blackthorn blossoms were fragile pledges;
Take the dogs, a basket, a walking stick.

Trophies to find on pleasant rambles,
The crab apple, sharp in its smooth, bright skin,
The luscious blackberries filched from brambles,
Bitter sloes yearning for sugar and gin.

Finders keepers for passing folk,
At West Green, Hound Green, Phoenix Green;
Along the canal towards Basingstoke,
Or at favourite places in between.

Homeward, laden down with treasures –
But looking forward, we must confess,
To the king of all local harvest pleasures –
Fresh trout, garnished with watercress.

WOODWIND

Autumn comes on, without hurry.
Leaves quietly ripen to glory,
Day after day, in the sunshine,
And in the cold radiance of starlight
And burning frosts, night after night.
Enchanted, the world slows its turning.
Trees gaze at changing reflections
Mirrored in glimmering water.
Without a soul there to record it,
Into the pricked ears of silence
A light breeze begins to play, solo,

Its delicate flute. Now an oboe,
A clarinet. Now all the woodwind
Performs a lively allegro,
Waves slap and hiss on the foreshore,
Accentuating the rhythm –
And all the trees burst out singing
In showers of coloured confetti.

OFF THE PEG

The guns in their places, strung out, carefully spaced,
Are actors and audience as the pageant unfolds,
Precisely choreographed. An expectant hush;
Until, from a distance, beaters advance in a line,
Clumping through woodland, chirruping wake-up calls.
Sticks thump on tree trunks, thrash at tangled briars
In ritual rhythm, like the pump of a heart.
High overhead, above it all, from the gods,
Buzzards mew sadly, most plaintive of predators.
Songbirds are sighted, flitting out from the trees;
Finches in small clouds twitter across the field,
Dancing like midges. Blackbirds. A blundering owl.
A high pigeon, tricky and tempting target. Not yet!
A deer in full flight appears – stops dead – hesitates –
Bewildered, facing silent, immobile men;
    Graceful even in terror, it exits, left.
    Offstage in the wings, reading between the lines,
    A kestrel hovers, scanning a scribbled hedge,
    And punctuates the blank page of the sky,
    A bold and aberrant apostrophe.
    And now the pheasants and the guns engage.

CLEMSFOLD ROUNDABOUT

Those three trees planted where the three roads meet,
Bare-branched all winter and all summer green,
When autumn comes quite suddenly catch fire
And leap into their own flamboyant dance:
Of all the trees in Sussex the only trees.
Crimson, orange and scarlet from head to heel,
Each polished performer sets the world ablaze,
Swirls to the rhythm of the shortening days,
Flaunting its beauty to the wind and rain –
Till laughing, breathless, spinning in its place
It drops its gleaming colours to the grass
As the next dancer takes up centre stage:
Of all the trees in Sussex the only tree.

OCTOBER DAY

As morning gathers strength, the mist retreats,
At first unveiling only a patch of ground
Scattered with acorns and crisp, golden leaves,
Then, foot by foot, the parent oak, stock still,
Its head lost in the clouds. Small shrubs emerge,
Freed by pale sunlight bravely filtering down.
Next, the green door. Two drakes on a sweep of lawn,
Walking together down towards the lake.
Beyond it, the red tree, like a barn ablaze.
And now – enough. The mist will yield no more.
It lingers in the fields, hangs in the wood,
Mysterious, noiseless, drifting like fine spray
About the green cascading willow tree.

HAND IN GLOVE

We're hand in glove, my winter coat and I
Now autumn's fires are quenched and blown away
And lingering brightness blotted from the sky,
And the whole chilly world is coloured grey.

My winter coat, drowsing all summer long
Safe in its cupboard, needs no warning shake:
At my first touch – together we belong –
It hugs me warmly, instantly awake.

Boots must jump to it, pull themselves together –
My coat and I will lead them quite a dance.
Ready? Come, stir your stumps, go hell for leather,
Your best foot forward now you have the chance.

Mittens curled up in pockets, fast asleep,
Sheepishly yawn and stretch, blink in the light;
A handkerchief-in-waiting takes a peep,
Sniffing the sharp air after a dreamless night.

The sun hangs in the mists, a crimson lamp;
Jackdaws and squirrels watch us as we pass,
Swinging our cheerful way through cold and damp
And leaving green footprints in the frosted grass.

Postcard from Wincanton

When Mrs P. zigzags out of her drive,
Clashing her gears with a hideous din,
In an urgent effort to help them survive,
Her neighbours snatch children and animals in.

FIELDS IN WINTER

No work in hand. Half comatose with cold,
Sloped fields lie silent under frost-bleached grass
Without a voice to murmur a complaint;
Only the borrowed creaking of a gate,
The owls, the vixen calling from the hill,
The borrowed long, long sighing of the wind.
Irregularly, ice cracks in the night
In frozen ditches, ticking away the time.
Indifferent host to ragged flocks of birds,
The land withdraws itself from dreary days
To meditate on deep, primeval fires
Flaming like suns at earth's most secret core,
Where molten rock runs hot through hidden veins,
Golden and bright; and winter never comes.

WINTER TREES

Alert, alive and listening to the wind,
Their autumn motley long since tossed away,
Lone standing trees display fine silhouettes –
An oak for all oaks, a very prince of poplars –
Each in its own space free to be itself.
In brindled fawns and umbers, snuffs and greys,
The woods beyond the hill wear winter furs
Flung boldly over tweedy, homespun bark.
With simple lures – a nest, a broken branch,
One last small cluster of remaining leaves –
They trap stray shafts of winter-pallid light,

Entangle them, make them linger, let them go.
Long roots thrust deep beneath the frozen clay,
They relish all weathers, bitter sleets and frosts,
Sing mightily in wild, uplifting gales
And hush for the still enchantment of the snow.

FROZEN SKIES OVER GATWICK
(Take-off and Stacking)

The grey sky turns white, frozen hard from horizon to rim,
A bleak, unwelcoming waste; but, undaunted, the planes
Put on their skates to crisscross the vast, hostile spaces.
Occasional travellers, keeping themselves to themselves,
With neither time nor desire to indulge in delays,
Follow a straight course, intent on their weighty affairs,
And trace whiter lines on their way across the pale ice.
More sociable, sporting companions remain on the scene
To spiral and circle and weave, thick as bees at the hive,
Passing, surpassing each other, observing the rules
Signalled by watchful, invisible men in control towers:
No smoking. No jostling. No horseplay. No aerobatics.
They dart and turn, skilfully wheeling, with never a pause,
Never a stumble. As darkness comes, all show their lights,
Making it easy to follow where each skater goes –
Till he glides away, heading for home or some far rainbow's end.

Postcard from Box Hill

It was icy, treacherous outside the pub
Where we stopped for a sandwich, a glass of wine.
In a shaft of pale sunshine, one frosted shrub,
Flaunting its jewels, made the whole day shine.

WHITE TULIPS

White tulips in a simple jar
Banish winter's lingering gloom;
Your flowers – and how like you they are –
At once illuminate a room.

Too soft for ear to hear it, yet
To gentle chamber music – strings,
Harp and flute and clarinet –
The listening house wakes up and sings.

A song of your shadow on the wall,
The air of friendly calm, the style,
The adventurous spirit; most of all
Your courage, and the unconquered smile.

FEBRUARY

After the long and weary wait –
Earth frozen hard, sky dark as slate –
Today a mild warmth was in the air,
And though the branches still were bare,
Birds whistled of Spring in every tree.
After heavy storms a quiet sea –
And stars flower profusely in the night,
Scattered narcissus, gold and white,
Leaning, each one, with conscious grace,
To gaze at its own reflected face,
Enthralled, and yearning to possess
That mirrored, perfect loveliness.

TAKE A DOZEN EGGS

A soufflé is a glorious thing, flirtatious and capricious;
Orange or cheese or chocolate, it looks and tastes delicious.
A thing so light and airy should never be a worry –
Enjoy the preparation and don't be in a hurry.
Line the dish with paper? This tip's worth many a dollar:
Tie buttered paper *outside*, so you can remove the collar.
Eggs and butter, flour and milk – so many delights!
Separate eggs carefully – get no yolk in with the whites;
If your hand slips, that's no problem, just put that one aside
For use as glaze, or omelette, whatever you decide.
Follow the steps, and in good time, call your guests to take a seat,
If it is to be served hot, this gorgeous, gourmet treat.
Now – here's a treasured secret, and only for your eyes:
Chill the egg whites in the freezer. This will make your soufflé rise
And rise – and rise – and rise – and rise
Beyond your wildest dreams, amazing all beholders!

RETURN OF THE REDHOT POKER

Even garden plants go in and out of fashion,
to be greeted with approval or a frown,
like dahlias, loved or loathed with equal passion –
But don't dream of cutting the rhododendrons down.

Fondly remembered, vanished childhood flowers –
snapdragons, lupins, marigolds – all these
have reappeared. But come sunshine, hail or showers –
Don't suggest uprooting our hydrangeas, please.

FOCUSED

He looks grave and intent, as if clad in rich priestly robes,
Though wearing the much-loved ancient and elbowless sweater
Under that terrible jacket; muddy boots, unspeakable trousers,
And a battered, despondent but faithful weatherproof hat.
His attention is wholly absorbed in tending the fire:
Oak and ash burning superbly at the red-orange heart,
Hungry flames briskly consuming the mountains of leaves,
Harvest of half a day's work. An old section of fence
Flares up, producing fierce heat; blue devils lick at bent nails.
Blazing pine logs emit fusillades of reports,
Sending, repeatedly, volleys of sparks in the air,
And oozing, like slow-moving lava, the bright molten sap.
Woodsmoke smells good as new bread freshly out of the oven
But makes the eyes water and sting in sly gusts of the breeze;
It wreathes and clings in the hair, in the clothes, in the gloves.
At length the sun reaches its goal and sets light to the sky,
Igniting a fiery furnace of breath-taking power;
Time to rake and bank up the bonfire, making it safe
To burn on, a living thing, out in the deepening dusk.
He picks up the chocolate wrappers, his half-empty mug,
Leaves his patient boots waiting outside, and steps quickly indoors.

Postcard from Salperton

On an open hillside an unknown tree
Painted itself on my memory's eye.
Perfectly shaped it appeared to me,
Graceful against the winter sky.

CHRISTMAS TREE

Let's move the hall table and bring in the tree –
even taller, more shapely than ever, I see.
Hoist it up slowly – the trunk must be straight –
now anchor it, so it supports its own weight.
A tree like this would make a beautiful mast
No ladder required. The staircase climbs past
so it's all within reach of the youngest, the smallest,
and the Average Person, not only the tallest.
First the Umpire arranges his twinkling lights,
all tested and working. Now for the delights
of finding and hanging our favourite things:
red apples, jewelled baubles, and five golden rings,
whole hosts of angels, a heavenly choir,
a birdcage, a penguin in festive attire,
a musical manuscript tied with a bow,
bells – stars – a little house covered in snow . . .
The mince pies smell wonderful. Here is the stable
and the crib figures – careful – to go on the table.
Umpire's inspection! I'm sure he'll agree
it exceeds expectations – and then we'll have tea.

HALF MOON AT KIRDFORD

I cannot remember a less friendly night;
The rain fell like whiplashes glimpsed in the light,
Chastising the garden, the cowering trees;
Just the evening to lounge here at home, at our ease –
  But we'd promised to meet you in Kirdford.

Roman Woods ran with water across the main road;
Streams snatched at our wheels; the fields overflowed,
And angling brambles fished round their edges,
Strung out in a ghostly row, blown from the hedges
  As we set out to join you in Kirdford.

Black roads and black floods from all the drowned ditches;
A wild night, too pitch dark for burglars or witches,
And too wet for ducks; teeming torrents of rain
As we took a wrong turning again and again,
  Determined to press on to Kirdford.

The heavenly host must have helped us survive;
Exhausted and late, a relief to arrive;
We dashed for the door, once parked under the sign –
And found you both, smiling and pouring the wine:
  Here we were, all together in Kirdford.

We were warmed through by the welcoming fire
And exchanged all the news while the bright flames leapt higher;
Now quite relaxed, in convivial mood,
We laughed and selected delectable food,
  Enjoying the good life in Kirdford.

When at last we emerged, one more pleasant surprise –
A half moon came out as we said our goodbyes;
Hugs and kisses all round, the skies starting to clear,
You'd been brilliant company, full of good cheer:
  What a great idea, meeting in Kirdford.

DAWN CHORUS

No question of drifting off to sleep again:
The birds are singing as the low mists clear,
Revealing a sampler of the day just born,
Stitched with a bumblebee, a butterfly,
A green and yellow woodpecker, a wren.
A masterpiece of detail and design –
Squirrels, a jackdaw with a sequin eye,
Twelve pigeons wheeling in a straggling line,
Foxgloves, tall feathered grasses, and a deer
Couched in the kingcups like a unicorn.

NEW LEAF

Grown old or simply blown down in a gale,
We have lost trees over the years.
One tall pine snapped off, halving its height,
And buried its javelin deep in the grass;
A silver birch, roots washed out by driving rain,
Collapsed gracefully on to a main power line:
Instant sabotage. We arrived home
To find Stygian darkness for miles around
While the family trailed candle wax all round the house.
We have planted an orchard and one walnut tree –
Harvesting squirrels enjoy all the nuts –
A maple that flames like a torch in October,
Crab apples, laburnum, a gingko tree, beech –
And horse chestnuts, one white, another dark pink,
Which light up their candles for you every Spring,
Celebrating your birthday with style and panache.

CROWS AND THEIR CRONIES

Much of a size and much of a feather,
Crows and their cronies may flock together.
They're mostly black. Their cries are hoarse,
Their habits appalling, their manners coarse.
They swagger about on sinewy legs,
Eat carrion, seeds, young birds and eggs –
Yet, once in the air, their graceful flight
Makes a surprisingly pleasing sight.
Observe the feather-fingered crow,
Soaring high and skimming low;
He swoops about with careless ease,
Builds lofty villages in trees
And stays alert for man's attack.
His jackdaw cousin's cry is "Chack!"
Grey-hooded, with a neat black cap,
He's an energetic, busy chap,
Another acrobat on wings;
His grey eye is caught by glittering things.
The magpie, elegantly dressed
In black and white, outshines the rest,
Flaunting an iridescent sheen
In subtle tones of blue and green.
No mystic powers – don't waste your time
Chanting some superstitious rhyme;
His influence upon your luck
Is nil, like that of any duck.
To fear a portent is absurd –
He's just a stylish, greedy bird.
The jay is colourful but shy,
Nervous, wary, ready to fly;
Moustached, he's pink, bright blue and grey;
One movement and he'll glide away.
Most of these birds are thieves and mockers.

The rook wears feathered knickerbockers
Yet is not mocked: that dagger beak
Could peck them into Wednesday week.
Bare-faced and larger than the crow,
His walk is confident and slow.
Largest of all, the raven's habits
Include sky-diving and poaching rabbits.
Sharper than any bird alive,
Come drought or flood, he will survive.
His rolling gait is rather strange,
Like his loud call: "Kronk!" He likes to range
Over rocky coasts and through mountain air –
But visit the Tower, you'll find him there.
Choughs play about in raucous gangs
By seaside cliffs and overhangs;
They're black, like crows, but overhead
You'll see their legs and beaks are red.
(The Alpine chough, their closest fellow,
Has legs of pink and a beak of yellow.)
Well, now I feel you've heard enough
To distinguish a jackdaw from a chough,
And to tell a crow from a passing rook,
Without recourse to a heavy book.
Now try to believe (you may well fail)
That only one half of them is male.

Postcard from Greece

Not a wasted journey. A cool peace reigned
When we reached the olive grove, you and I.
The gates to the ruins were locked and chained,
But nightingales sang. No one else came by.

BACK ROAD TO WARNHAM

The back road to Warnham is winding and blessedly green,
But hazardous, too, you will find. Occasional cars
Come scorching round bends, each the only car in its world,
Each racing against its own record, set two days ago;
So sharpen your wits and your senses, and mind how you go
Uphill and down, through mysterious tunnels of trees.
In season, look out for wild garlic in delicate flower
And, in season, the small tree whose rounded leaves turn to
fine gold,
Dropping like pennies from heaven. Once, to my surprise,
A kilo of feathers was dashed to the ground just ahead –
A sparrowhawk taking a pigeon: a bolt from the blue.
Once – was he deaf, or simply feeling unfriendly? –
Minding his business, without so much as a glance,
A badger lumbered across and off into the hedge.
He wore baggy, ill-fitting trousers, unlovely but warm,
Earth-stained but rainproof; no doubt the one pair to his name,
Kept up, I supposed, by a length of old baler twine.
He may wear them a year or two yet, given reasonable care,
Nosing for slugs in the bluebells, or under a patch
Of bright yellow dandelion sunbursts and misty pale moons.

TAYLOR AT LEAMINGTON SPA

Relaxed and graceful – but so near the edge –
A pretty little tortoiseshell, asleep
On an upper outside window ledge:
Angels and men, were she to fall, would weep.

Safer than on a chair or friendly mat,
She basks, unseen by monsters she hides from –
Ginger George, the much-feared Dratted Cat,
And Stripey Sam, Black Bismark and Great Tom.

They brawl and swagger, conquerors of the earth,
Shouldering in through catflaps not their own,
Raping and pillaging for all they're worth,
And not disposed to leave the young alone.

So here she slumbers, well beyond their reach;
Sophisticated feline she is not,
But her warm fur smells wholesome as a peach,
And on her cheek she wears a beauty spot.

BLUEBELLS

Among the trees, great drifts of blue
Like wood smoke; sunlight dappling through.
A place to sit and think of you.

The air is kind, the sky is clear;
A lovely, healing time of year.
The pain is over, and the fear.

New life is springing. Grace-notes fall
From branches where small songbirds call.
Time passes gently, if at all.

Past and present quietly meet,
And memories bloom, rich and sweet
As bluebells growing at my feet.

Among the trees, great drifts of blue
Like wood smoke; sunlight dappling through.
A place to sit and think of you.

THE ORGANIST

The sheep in their pews gaze before them, not off to one side
Where I, in my hidden pride, know is the true seat of power,
Were the mitred Bishop himself enthroned in the sanctuary.
A click, quiet hum, then the music flowers under my fingers.
They all move like puppets on strings at my music's bidding,
Kneeling or standing, obedient, singing or silent,
And I punish the Vicar, make him practise the patience he
                                               preaches
For sixteen slow bars, while humbly he waits at the altar.
Unseen, I survey the flock awaiting my signal.
Why do they think they are here, foregoing their freedom,
Sunday by Sunday? Not for the badly-read sermon. No,
Only for me, to surrender themselves to my orders.
Mine is the thunder, the glory, the voice of the angels.
At will I could stun them, drown them in floodwaves of sound,
But I spare them; make them aware of the force and the fury
Kept dammed, and let them go, grateful, into the morning air.

NOCTURNE

Midnight was solemnly struck. The clock, duty done,
Faces less weighty demands for several hours;
It chimes one quiet note; and then two, more or less to itself.
Outside, moonlight fitfully gleams on the slumbering lake;
Each little while, owls exchange coded news of the hunt;
The roads are all empty and silent; the world is asleep.
Let the sleeping world lie, its intrusive affairs
Cease to nag at the mind in the sheltering dark.
The whole clutter of unanswered letters and telephone calls,
Jobs to be done and concerns to confront and resolve,
Can be put aside, wait their turn until morning has come.
This is the time to dip into the bright treasure-store

Kept hidden and safe in the undisturbed cupboards of night;
Memories, real or imagined, old secrets and dreams
To sift through the fingers with pleasure untinged with regret.
I hear songs in a language whose lovely words fall like soft rain –
Warm summer seas wash on faraway sands at my feet –
Sun sparkles on trees cased in ice to the tip of each branch –
Pink roses bloom in the angle of ancient stone walls –
Firelight flickers on furnishings, chintz, rich brocades –
Paradise birds plunder fruit from familiar gardens –
Here is my old magic carpet, winged horses to ride –
Here, wreathing like incense-smoke, breathed in unheeded, is sleep.

BARLEYSUGAR, THE HANDSOME CAT

Let other felines keep warm, grow fat,
Quite contented to stay at home;
Barleysugar, that handsome cat,
Prefers to be free to hunt and roam.

He earns his living with practised skill –
Young rabbits, voles, mice in a drain –
And quarters the fields, the gardens, the hill
Selected by him as his domain.

He's self-sufficient and wide awake,
Sometimes seen basking in the sun,
Or stalking intently along the lake,
Unbeholden to anyone.

The night belongs to him, and the day;
Owls and squirrels leave him alone,
And even foxes will turn away –
For Barleysugar can hold his own.

DIGITAL CLOCK

The digital clock has been there in the kitchen for years
Controlling hot water and heating all over the house
And coming in handy for telling the time as I cook –
But since the New Year it has taken on life of its own.
The numbers have all become dates after 7 p.m.
As I switch on the oven it's 1906, 07, 08 and 09:
Dates of the Ancestors' births. The World Wars creep up
While I slice the peppers and mushrooms: 1914 – 18
Four years of terror and tragedy, over in moments
But reflected on, fleetingly, daily. This good olive oil
Is better than that last small bottle. More expensive, of course.
You pour me a glass of white wine as our parents are courting
And marry. Your birthday year now, and mine shortly after
If I should happen to look. 1940's a sobering moment –
All the lights out, and only one egg per person per week –
But life going on, a brother and sisters, and gas masks
And sunshine and skipping ropes, normal as bombs in the night
And normal as sleeping in bunk beds under the stairs.
Will you answer the phone? I'm all floury, but say I'll ring back.
1951 and the salmon is done to a turn. We still haven't met
But I'll love you the minute I see you. The table is laid,
Is everyone ready for supper? 1959
And our marriage. Life's great new adventure –
But before I can blink, 2000, 2001…
Forty years, gone like that: all the joys and the griefs and the
Journeys,
The places, the babies, the friends and the books and the wine,
The dancing and packing and Christmas cards – gone at a stroke.
How like life – and the digital clock does not even tick.

THE FOX

Suave and relaxed, sometimes pausing to sniff at a flower,
And not unaware that he causes a bit of a stir,
The fox appears early each morning to stroll on the grass.
He is rather expensively dressed for the time and the place
But too neatly groomed, one would swear, to have been out all night,
Up to no good, or painting the chicken-run red.
Unlike other creatures, sporting his brushed, russet coat,
He seems landowner rather than peasant, in a different class
From the frivolous squirrels, the short-sighted, hardworking mole,
The leaderless rabble of rabbits, the unspeakable stoat.
Cold-hearted, his critics say, greedy, disreputable.
Perhaps. He has style, a certain self-confident grace
And has done me no harm. I take pleasure in seeing him pass,
Making his way past the oak tree about his affairs.

SUSSEX MORNING

Morning shines bright on the meadow I see from my window
Getting on with the day before anyone starts to take notice.
Sheep graze, woolly and black faced, at ease with each other;
High in the ash tree the crows are attending a meeting
And small birds are busily singing along all the hedges.
There are so many ducklings they have to line up to be counted,
So many rabbits they cannot be counted at all –
And sometimes, long legged and graceful, appearing from nowhere,
Shamelessly thirsting for roses, the trespassing deer.

MOONSTREAM

Once in a while, undesired, undeserved,
moonlight pours in, flooding the quiet house.
Pure and clear, filtered through branches and closewoven vines,
it washes, caresses cool windows, seeking its level,
pooling on polished wood, soaking, submerging the shadows,
steadily filling to brimming the unshuttered rooms,
all hushed, all enchanted, all glimmering, all bleached to silver.
Mirrors watch spellbound, unblinking. In shoals, flank to flank,
shoes hang motionless, weightless, nose to the current,
dark bristled sea-urchin hairbrushes cling to pale surfaces . . .
Downstairs a clock sometimes chimes, a few fathoms below.
Then, in its sleep, the world turns, hunching a shoulder,
diverting the moonstream elsewhere . . . and the light
fades, dries, evaporates . . . dreamlike, is utterly gone.

COUNTRY POSTMAN, WITH NEWSPAPER

A glimpse of Eden's bliss before the fall!
Seated on the pavement in the sun,
His back against the warm bricks of the wall,
Newspaper spread wide. Has his side won?

Above his head , a postbox. In the frame
His post van waits, its bodywork agleam,
Scarlet and gold, while he relives the game
In black and white, the colours of his team.

He takes his ease, unconscious of my gaze
And quite untroubled by a speck of dirt;
Fit uniform for these informal days:
Navy shorts and sky blue, short sleeved shirt.

OPEN WINDOWS

Sighing its satisfaction, the house breathes in summer
through wide open windows. Curtains billow and float
in somnolent bedrooms enjoying a long afternoon.
Ladybirds, flies and the scents of wisteria and roses
wash in and out as the gentle breeze rises and falls,
or are swept off downstream to make landfall in backwater
                                                    bathrooms.
The sitting room, quietly deserted, unnaturally tidy,
devoid of the plants moved outside to a place in the shade,
sees as the sun picks out book titles, gilds an armchair.
The dining room relishes calm, smelling faintly of polish;
and the chairs might embark on a light-hearted holiday dance
were it not for the chance that someone might open the door,
looking for spoons, or for sugar to sift on the strawberries.
The cool kitchen thrums to the sound of the washing machine
and the dryer, both constantly busy. Still more damp towels
await their turn for a tumble. Among china jugs,
bees bumbling in from the terrace on course for the hive,
weighed down with nectar, dizzy and fuddled with sweetness,
are trapped and have to be rescued, sent on their way.
The house, smiling, settles itself in a comfortable pose,
creaking a little, aware of all this and much more –
a slight fall of soot, the car-keys lost deep in a sofa –
but concentrating its mind on the green smell of grass,
the warmth of the day, the sum of the pleasures of summer.

IMPROMPTU

Who threw the pebble out into the lake,
Startling the surface abruptly awake?
Circular patterns spread, silver and black,
Cross and crisscross themselves, cannoning back,
Ruffling reflections and feathering ferns.
As each liquid furrow retires and returns;
Ripples retreat and fresh ripples advance,
Measure for measure, in intricate dance . . .
The movement is slowing now. Rank follows rank
To slide behind curtains of leaves by the bank,
Losing all purpose of travelling on;
All that energy spent; all that impetus gone.
Was it a stone? A fish after a fly?
The water lies calm and still, smooth as the sky.

TENNIS, ANYONE?

Somehow our Saturday mornings run to extremes.
Breakfast continues for hours. Piles of washing appear.
Glorious scents of hot coffee and toast fill the air,
While shampoos and showers flow on unabated, upstairs.
Earliest risers come in for more coffee, a chat,
After going off to buy newspapers , more eggs and milk.
The telephone's ringing – shout if it's someone for me.
I've found one gold earring. Has somebody got my blue shirt?
Are the Ancestors coming tomorrow? The Rector as well?
We shall need one more leaf in the table and possibly two.
That load is just finishing, yours can be next if you like.
Did they do a good job on the mower? The post has arrived –
Some wonderful stamps on your letter, whoever it's from.
Good morning, darling! The kettle is just on the boil . . .

TOTAL ECLIPSE

In Cornwall, teeming rain. They photographed the dark,
Splintered by camera flashes. No glimpse of sun or moon,
Both totally eclipsed behind dense cloud. At sea,
In between downpours, hauling on the sheets,
Splicing the mainbrace, dodging other craft,
I'm sure they saw it. Some of them, at least,
Saw parts of it, at least. On a perfect summer day,
I was busy in the garden with a trowel;
Eleventh-hour sun was fiercely hot – and then
Began to cool and fade. The birds fell silent.
Sunshine dimmed to a clear, subaqueous green.
At various heights, incredibly far above,
Miniscule silver planes sped through the sky.
Long minutes of strange magic. A cautious glance:
The sun was gone, but for a fiery fringe.
The air grew warmer as the light grew bright,
Birds sang, and squirrels bounded about the trees.
Ever since, they've told me: "Sussex? No!
You certainly won't have witnessed full eclipse."

HEDGEROW

Honeysuckle white and yellow,
Honeysuckle pink and red;
A thrush out-sings its nearest fellow,
Larks pipe descants overhead.

Blackthorn, whitethorn, morning glory,
A nest, an ash-tree hung with keys;
Butterflies and stinging-nettles,
Wasps and ladybirds and bees.

Hips and haws and elderberries,
Deadly nightshade in between;
Vigorously rampant brambles,
Fruiting crimson, black and green.

Blackbirds warble, rich and mellow,
A spider weaves its shining thread;
Honeysuckle white and yellow,
 Honeysuckle pink and red.

DREAM

I dreamed the marriage of the moon and sun
In the warm sky filled with their tender light:
The moon composed but blushing apricot,
The sun softly dimmed to lemon, as a guest
Invited, this once, into the watching night.
Calm and serene they took their ritual way
Until the two circles touched and came to rest,
Shining.
 I saw, and the world saw, satisfied,
 Before like a song the dream came to an end,
 Neither sun nor moon at all eclipsed.

POSTCARD from Chausey

A great little island! Everyone feels
We should stay here longer – it's not up to me.
We eat fresh fish and oysters. Convivial meals.
And always, as background, the sound of the sea.

BACHELOR BIRD

(fringilla coelebs)

Those of you speaking bird Latin
May have asked yourselves – as have I –
Why the chirpy and colourful chaffinch
Was named Bachelor Finch. This is why.

When winter approaches, the chaffinch
Sees off his wife and brood
To migrate to far destinations,
Leaving him plenty of food.

In your hospitable garden
Only the male will be seen –
Until, storm-tossed but plucky and punctual,
Spring greets the return of his queen.

Then his song becomes loud and triumphant,
His plumage well-preened – a delight;
He dazzles his drab little partner,
And is eager and ready to fight.

He attacks any window at daybreak,
Seeing himself mirrored there,
Determined to oust the intruder,
And madder than any March hare.

Brawling and singing and flirting,
His existence is great beyond words:
The chaffinch, fringilla coelebs,
From a long line of bachelor birds.

GARDEN IN THE DARK

Away from lighted windows, the dark closes in.
Over the town, grey clouds lit from below
Form a thin, woollen blanket, stained orange-pink.
Further west, pale stars are scattered. No moon tonight.
It dwindled of course, as always, that great shining disc
Trimmed to a sliver of lemon, to a fingernail paring –
But no moon at all seems odd, puts the night out of joint.
Hearing and touch take over as principal guides,
Sight resigning its role with no very good grace.
Twice a fox barks, sharp and cold. An unidentified bird,
Alarmed by my stillness, makes me start in my turn,
Blundering out of the dark pines over my head.
Friendly bushes rustle in unfriendly fashion.
I grasp at the handrail to see me over the bridge ,
Its calm wooden strength affording me fresh confidence.
The willow, quietly standing on the far bank,
Trails its long patient fingers in the black water,
Sifting for precious, all but invisible fragments
As they tumble, glinting, down to the mud at the bottom;
Dimmed, broken pieces which once, whole, made the bright
moon.

OAK

The many oak trees, older than the house,
provide abundant acorns, generous shade –
and heaps of logs when one lets fall a branch.
Each is a wildlife haven for all the birds –
including sparrowhawks – and squirrels. One
has its own title: it is called The Oak.

OPEN HOUSE

A friendly house. It delights in company,
Likes its bones warmed, likes voices in every room,
Enormous meals, and kettles on the boil,
Laughter, chat, smells of coffee and shampoo,
Windows and doors set wide in sunny weather,
Roaring log fires when evenings turn chill.
No fuss, no frenzy, no rota for washing up,
No fixed times for breakfast or close of play.
Play the piano, emerge from your shell and sing,
Amuse the Ancestors with travellers' tales,
Take long walks, borrow any book you choose.
Trains can be met at any time of day –
But no presents, please: the pleasure is all ours.

THE ROSE

Not a pallid imitation. This is my kind of rose –
As touching in its perfection as any that ever bloomed –
No pampered, scentless confection fit only for flower shows,
But gorgeous, in blazing colour and headily perfumed.

Vibrant, deep-hearted beauty, sprung from the homely clay,
Radiant, and dancing with every breeze that blows,
Each bud another promise, unfolding day by day –
The real thing, thorns and all. Now that's what I call a rose.

SUMMER NIGHT

Don't go away now the dew is falling –
We have to save each other from the foggy, foggy dew;
Don't leave me while the owls are calling –
Their lonely calling makes me lonely for you.

I can't let you go while the moon is rising,
So far, so cold – I need you, warm and near;
Please stay with me; the world is so surprising
But I can't pay attention unless you are here.

Hold my hand while the stars are burning,
Wheeling and shining in the midnight sky.
Let's stand together as the universe is turning
And half a dozen comets rush cavorting by.

The night is too beautiful to think of sleeping,
And the whole taste of summer is in your kiss.
It would be madness to part before tomorrow comes creeping,
For there probably will never be another night like this.

THE POPPY

Young and flamboyant, dazzling the sun
In a dramatic swirl of scarlet silk,
She took me – and the garden – by surprise;
In the dewy freshness of the morning,
She leapt unruffled, ravishing and free
From the green, compact, enclosing bud.
Beside himself, the bumble bee, far from humble,
Set about burrowing deep into unplumbed nectar,
Lost to all else but pillaging and plunder.

THE ORCHID

If my loved ones are flowers,
Among them you are the orchid in full bloom,
Elegant. Fine. The upward-springing stems
Look fragile, but are resilient and strong.
Delicate blossoms, blond to bronze champagne,
Conceal in their airy grace self-discipline,
A will of steel, a honed intelligence,
A loving heart, a most delightful wit –
And carry a subtle trace of your perfume.

CUPID DISARMED

Love, I have never done you wrong –
Why threaten me with pointed arrow?
You are not blind, but bold and strong,
And wicked mischief to the marrow.
Fire darts into some idle throng
Where plenty of hearts are lying fallow!
I'll buy your indulgence with a song,
Since my heart is not yours to harrow.

Sad songs are two or three a penny,
Pouring out from all directions,
From Zanzibar to Abergavenny,
Bewailing the loved one's cold rejections;
Sad songs from every John and Jenny –
But where are your graceful, light confections,
Happy songs – have you so many? –
Singing requited love's perfections?

In praise of a love that lasts forever,
I can weave you a song of such delight
The listening rocks will quake and shiver,
The hunting owl pause in its flight,
The fish leap from the spell-bound river,
The moon forget to sail the night . . .
Unstring your bow. Put down your quiver:
Now pass me my pen, and let me write.

THE OTHER HOUSE

Nowhere near here, and up a rutted track,
We saw – and nearly bought – a different house,
A cleverly converted long, low barn,
Old and attractive. On the small side for us –
Ample room for a family of four
With only one ancestor. No further room.
The garden was pleasant, quiet, a rectangle
Carved from a big estate, and mostly lawn
With, at one side, a lovely swimming-pool,
And thoroughbred horses grazed beyond the fence.
It lacked places to wander, doing childish things
Unobserved from the windows on each floor –
Talking to made-up friends or Robin Hood,
Trying to make a fire by rubbing sticks,
Blowing dandelion clocks and wasting time,
Getting stung by wasps and falling out of trees,
Playing dangerous and pointless games.
Might that house, once ours, have tamed us all?
Imposed a calmer, neater, more serious style?
That we can only guess, but will never know:
That house – or we ourselves – got clean away.

HOME or AWAY

THE ACOLYTE

Seated close by the piano, dressed all in black,
as if to be less than a presence, invisible even,
the acolyte is there to serve without being seen;
but the lights, though angled to shine on the ivory keys
and the pianist's strong, supple fingers, cast gleams on her too,
on the burnished gold hair, the steady, unwavering gaze –
The face of a warrior angel, calm and intent.
Always precise to a second, not missing a beat,
without hesitation or fumbling, her eyes on the score,
the acolyte, deft, unobtrusive, turns over a page.
The music ripples and trips, skips, meanders and flows,
increasing in volume, a small stream becoming a river,
solemn and stately, gathering strength as it goes,
then crashing, majestic, over precipitous falls
before, at last, finding its way to the welcoming floods,
and losing itself in the wide, in the infinite sea . . .
Silence, for several heartbeats. Then storms of applause.
The pianist stands, bows and smiles, bows and modestly smiles –
And now the acolyte stirs, clapping and clapping and clapping.

A FINE DAY

Suddenly all the buses, picked out by shafts of sunshine,
Are carrying charming people to wonderful destinations;
Suddenly all the pigeons are white doves, wheeling and tumbling,
Headlines tell only good news; passersby smile at each other.
A warm light caresses the buildings. Flags never fluttered more bravely,
The grass is suddenly greener, the air itself clearer and kinder.
Fresh vigour sweeps through the city; and the tide comes surging upriver,
Dancing with boats as it passes, sparkling, and silver with fishes.

MAKING SHIFT

He danced barefoot and on an empty stage,
Slowly, gravely, totally alone:
Dancing, light and music all engage
To make such moments perfectly one's own.

He danced. The packed house was mere lofty space.
The lighting clear, so cunningly contrived
It fell like sunshine on his arms and face –
Then giant shadows, dancing too, arrived.

They danced, each separate and yet together,
Noiseless, disciplined, with vibrant zeal,
Mysteriously free from any tether
Holding them each a captive at his heel.

Only by shadows partnered and attended,
Intent upon the subtle game they played,
He danced, they danced, their comradeship unended
Until the ending of the serenade.

WINTER LIGHT

How I love these cold and shining days,
The rooftops burnished by slow-rising suns,
And all the ordinary passers by
Haloed in glory, buoyed up by the light,
All but afloat. Weightless, they advance
Along the shadowed pavements, silhouettes
Drifting with purpose in a waking dream;
Anonymous, their faces left in shade.

SPRINGTIME IN KENSINGTON GARDENS

The trees are explosions of joy across the park
A masterpiece each one, made for delight,
Blossoms and leaves erupting from branch and bark,
Fireworks in blazing colours, in brilliant white.

A display to set the Serpentine on fire,
A celebration fit to make us sing;
The touch-paper is lit, step back, admire
The wild exuberance of lovely Spring.

Still, that little willow I shall not forget,
Lit by pale sunshine, washed by recent rain,
Blown by the breeze: a young girl, long hair wet,
Modest and graceful, shaking it dry again.

MORNING COMES

Morning comes, gently but firmly. Rain slides down the roofs,
pit-patters on half-awake skylights, puts paid to sleep.
Slates glisten, blue-grey as pigeons in mating attire.
Gales in the night howled and lashed themselves into frenzy,
knocking off dustbin lids, clattering down in the street,
sobbing down chimney-pots, shrieking and banging at doors,
and dashing water like gravel against curtained panes.
Daylight and soft falling rain restore order together,
washing the city, the tired, tearstained face of the sky,
dissolving and rinsing away the torn remnants of dreams.
Light gleams on familiar windows, wet treetops and spires;
the everyday world is restored to us. Morning has come.

LINCOLN'S INN

June light will paint in watercolours,
Scenes of each familiar corner of the square.
Now, in the sharp, cold January sun,
(The few folk passing indicating scale),
The buildings mimic old prints of themselves,
Clear, uncluttered, unobscured by leaves,
The trees mere outlines, rapidly sketched in.
Well-ordered, unpretentious elegance;
A job well done. A lasting monument.
Long dead, the architect smiles in his sleep.

PRETTY GIRL

All the pretty girls look like you
When they first come into view,
Laughing and chatting without a care,
With their flirty skirts and their well-washed hair.
There is a resemblance, that much is true –
But they're none of them quite as pretty as you.

All the pretty girls look like you;
Some days I catch sight of one, sometimes two,
Swinging along with a cheerful smile,
Jackets and shoes in the latest style
And fingernails painted the latest hue –
But they never are quite as pretty as you.

All the pretty girls look like you –
The sun comes out and the skies turn blue,
Postmen are carrying wonderful things,
Dustmen are wearing white feathery wings –
But on closer inspection they just won't do:
To be properly pretty – they'd have to be you.

REFLECTIONS IN HARLEY STREET

Clean white stucco, balconied upper floors,
Opulent curtains in the latest style,
Gleaming brasswork, heavy, painted doors –
Odd numbers reflect the evens for half a mile.

A woman comes to the window across the street,
In the waiting room of number 99;
How odd it would be if our eyes should meet,
And her appearance clearly mirror mine . . .

No. Dark hair, glasses, heavy orange beads –
But she's a portrait from another age,
Posed by a master; calm and intent, she reads,
Catching the daylight on a tilted page.

I do not know her, but I wish her well.
Turning away in case I seem to stare,
I take my place, sea-creature in its shell,
Sitting and writing in a friendly chair.

ALBERT BRIDGE

Built, one might think, as a fantasy alone,
Designed to delight – the backdrop for a play –
An outrageous confection, conjured from iron and stone,
Airy-fairy, lighter than wind-blown spray.

But the swirling river wears it as a crown
Linking territories on either side,
Observed from vantage points, upstream and down –
Glass houses, piers, and boats borne on the tide.

And when the shades of night begin to fall,
An insubstantial dream, it hangs in space,
Decked out in glittering diamonds over all,
Its magic mirrored on the water's face.

STARLINGS

Times of performance will vary, according to season:
In winter, matinées only, at three or three-thirty;
In summer at eight, perhaps nine. Good family viewing.
A celebration of skill, of daylight and space.

Arriving expectantly, perching in rows close together,
In large or small parties or singly, as an audience will,
They jostle and chatter and preen in the sun's last warm rays,
Forming a musical score too dense to interpret.
Then, at some imperceptible signal, they are all transformed
Into airy performers, in a breathtaking, daily display
Of sheer virtuosity. Wave after wave, interweaving
With no hesitation or awkwardness, no ruffled feathers;
Whole symphonies, anthems, orchestrated arpeggios,
Spontaneous cadences, cunningly crafted concertos
Of flyaway notes, swooping and swirling in unison.
At last, section by section, glissando, they skim the pale river –
    And vanish –
        to settle on hidden staves under the bridges.

POSTCARD from Hyde Park

A portly bird with a tiny head,
Pompous waddle, mad white-rimmed eye,
Scruffy uniform: but all that said,
See magic unfold as wings reach for the sky.

HOME OR AWAY

When you are here, the world hums, unhurried, along.
Time dashes merrily by, all its harness-bells jingling,
Moons wax and wane as they ought, and the tides come and go;
Suns rise and set with a flourish, a neat pirouette –
Glance away, and it's Saturday week in a fraction of no time.
But without you, the universe changes; and not for the better.
Bright spring-heeled days go with you, to be poorly replaced
By dull, leaden-footed affairs. The slow sun hangs fire;
Discouraged, it ponders the stretch between daybreak and noon.
The hour hand toils round the clock, sadly measuring absence.
The sundial is silent. The postman's a pillar of salt.
The lively wind drops; flags crumple, unmotivated.
The rudderless moon floats adrift among uncharted clouds,
Tides wallow, lost and confounded, with nowhere to go.
Time weighs heavy on the hands, very heavy;
Time weighs so very heavy while you're gone.

UNKNOWN YOUNG MAN

Neatly and soberly dressed, but with long limbs a-sprawl,
He ignores the whole carriage, without gazing out at the view.
Unaware, or uncaring? Unfocused. Nothing to read.
Haircut fashionable, not outrageous. Nails bitten short.
Shoes slightly scuffed, could do with a smidgeon of polish.
Grey socks, concertinas, expose several inches of shin.
One presumes no identity crisis; but those socks are at odds,
Visibly marked with two different, unmatching names –
And the navy sweater, at a guess, sports yet a third.
Misleading claims; but, taken together, a clue
As to the station at which we shall see him alight.

BATTERSEA BRIDGE

Battersea Bridge is all buses and bustling
From morning to night, with vans jostling and hustling,
Colour and noise beyond any believing,
Bicycles swooping and dodging and weaving,
Lorries impatiently panting and growling,
Police cars in hunting packs yapping and howling,
Pedestrians, striding out, strolling and shambling,
People with dogs, marching briskly and ambling,
Ambulance crews on emergency missions,
Plumber and builders and cooks and technicians . . .
Traffic thins and disperses, the tempo slows down,
Neat taxis are heading for theatres in town,
secure in the Knowledge and sure of a fare;
They are lit now by golden lamps hanging in air.
The strong bridge, with its elegant arches, remains.
Its sibling upstream carries little toy trains.

THE THAMES

London's river, at all hours, any day,
At all states of the tide, come rain or shine,
Glittering silver, bronze or pewter grey:
Familiar, always changing, and always mine.

A brightly illustrated waking dream;
Pleasure-craft and barges come and go,
Merrily shoot through bridges with the stream,
Or labour, upriver or down, against the flow.

Herons and pigeons, mud between their toes,
Patrol the foreshore when low tide hangs slack.
Gulls dispute the territory with crows,
Skirmishing, swooping, gliding, white and black.

When starlings roost, boats moor and ducks take flight,
Joggers and cyclists trickle from the park.
A vivid sunset; then a gentler light
Caresses the water, dwindling into dark.

The river flows on, soothing the lonely hours,
Diluting harsh acrylic neon signs
To tender water-colours, reflected towers
To wavering, faint, ephemeral designs.

THE DANVERS STREET BLACKBIRD

In Danvers Street a bird is singing. Pause
And listen as he practises his song,
Intent and focused, seeking no applause,
But making his music supple, sweet and strong.

Surely the most ambitious of his kind,
He spends the short hours of the winter day
In any shaft of sunlight he can find,
Trilling and carolling the time away.

When Spring at last comes, he'll have become, by then,
The local hero with the golden voice;
He'll pick himself the right brown-feathered hen
And with her find a nesting-place of choice.

Perhaps he'll opt to glide down and install
His little lovebird in a secret nook,
Hidden from public gaze, at Crosby Hall;
Her preference may be for them to look
For somewhere near the royal thoroughfare,
In some bright-blossomed tree in Paultons Square.

THOROUGHFARES

Siren songs of police cars; the occasional grumble
Of heavy lorries at lights, lumbering on their way;
Familiar, unthreatening noises, a low background rumble
Like friendly voices conversing, all part of the day.

On the pavement, everyone moves in their own separate world-
Photographers, children, dogs, tourists, pushchairs and their likes;
Commuters determinedly shoulder ahead, brollies furled,
Defying the lawlessly swooping piratical bikes.

And the river, showing a placid face, follows its course,
A highway for boats of all sizes, loved and well-known.
Beautiful. Dangerous as an untameable horse,
Headstrong and wilful, obeying no laws but its own.

TRANSPORTED

It's a brisk and optimistic time of day,
Just after nine. The rush-hour has quietened down,
And traffic flows unimpeded over the bridge,
Along Beaufort Street towards Fulham, or the King's Road.
The buses are now far from crowded – too early for shoppers.
Young mothers and nannies ride scooters home along pavements,
Light-hearted and dashing, on their way back from school,
Lifting the spirits of men loading scaffolding poles.
People eat breakfast, drink coffee and smoke outside cafés,
Gesturing widely and gossiping into their phones.
My meeting is to take place far away across town.
I could catch a bus, then another to Waterloo Station
And walk from there, under the railway bridge, not very far –
Or simply stand here and wait until, sooner or later,
A black cab looking for hire draws up at the kerb

To whisk me efficiently off through the London I love,
Free to gaze at the scenery: Battersea Park,
Parliament Square, Lambeth Palace and the Old Vic,
Enriched by commentary in the familiar tones
Of one brought up east of the Tower or south of the Thames,
Streetwise and compassionate. Well, now, a difficult choice.

WORKING LUNCH

Exchange of hugs, and kisses in the air –
They look not unalike – the shoes, the hair;
A histrionic "I'm exhausted!" sigh.
And shopping bags are piled up, table high.

Glasses of wine; the latest word on Tim,
Holiday plans, and Mervyn at the gym.
Mock guilt, and happy smiles of satisfaction
Over trophies of the morning's stirring action.

Now lunch. They take the light and healthy choice –
Diet is mentioned, in a serious voice,
And sacrifices for one's figure's sake –
Then coffee, and a naughty slice of cake.

"I must dash! Jason has to see the vet."
"Let's fix a date, before we both forget."
"You'll let me know about Nick's situation?"
"Come on! Let's share a taxi to the station."

SWANSONG

Mute swans. Calm, unruffled, beautiful,
Sailing before the breeze along the river,
Totally unmoved by images
Floating beside them, mirroring perfection.
Proud heads turn regally, or bend with grace
On elegantly arching, supple necks.
Enraptured, Tchaikovsky calls out for his pen,
Manuscript paper and a glass of wine,
A corps de ballet and an orchestra.

From the towpath, Degas' analytic eye
Observes the ungainly scramble up the bank,
The cumbersome bodies, awkward, lurching gait,
Large, flat feet turned inwards. There they stand,
Lopsided, seemingly forlorn and lost,
Morosely preening their plumage. They are, for him,
A group of dancers in a dressing-room,
Each separate ugly duckling tying a shoe
Or tugging at the bodice of her dress.

As shadow-patterns suddenly slide past
And music loudly thrums, close overhead,
The child lifts startled eyes and drops her book.
Across the water-meadow, flying low,
Five swans are neatly spaced in line astern,
Beating time with wide, angelic wings.
Voiceless, they conjure rhythmic, haunting sounds
From their own feathers sweeping through the air,
A song without words accompanying their flight.

THE MARGAUX AS USUAL

Young men come and go from round the table –
Phone-calls to make and cigarettes to light;
The two girls, insofar as they are able,
Speak across empty chairs to left and right.

Expensive handbags, understated dresses;
Expensive shirts, of course without a tie;
Fine food, fine wines. Each detail coolly stresses
That money's made to burn, and fish to fry.

They boast of bonuses, discuss commission –
If someone else is talking, it's a bore;
Been there, done that, seen off the competition.
Good question, Rob! What *is* a heaven for?

THE PRINCE OF SOMMELIERS

Of arrogance or presumption, there's no trace.
Neatly groomed, immaculately dressed,
Alert for the slightest detail not in place,
He moves unhurriedly from guest to guest.

His courtesy seems natural, inborn;
He has a dignity beyond his years;
The symbols of his status, lightly worn,
Are recognized, respected by his peers.

He speaks five languages beside his own,
Yet few imagine, as they sit to dine,
The stubborn perseverance he has shown
To qualify him to pour out their wine.

CORNER TABLE

Always welcome guests. The waiter's pen
Is poised and ready in anticipation;
The table in the corner's set for ten,
And quiet enough for general conversation.

Menus surrendered, talk turns to the news:
New drugs, new regulations, the recession,
Politics, sport. They air their varied views
And wrangle amiably, without aggression.

Luigi himself appears with smiles, and stands
Chatting of opera with quiet animation,
Approving bright ties and steady, well-scrubbed hands –
And moderation, even in moderation.

DINNER AT THE OLIVE TREE

I saw her earlier – young, tall and thin,
Hair tightly held back in a ponytail,
Scarlet outfit sharp against a skin
Not meant to tan, but delicate, and pale.

Tables are set outside. A perfect night.
Her hair is loose now, softening her face;
Her eyes, enormous in the candlelight,
Smile as her companion takes his place.

No need of sorcery or magic ring.
Her voice is charming, with its Irish lilt,
As was Isolde's: fatal to Knight and King,
Even if the potion had been spilt.

THE WAITING GAME

Every one of our tables is taken –
We're wickedly busy tonight;
The kitchen is stirred but not shaken,
Though the chef seems geared up for a fight.

One woman stares hard at her neighbour
While forking in eggs Florentine;
Two girls are discussing New Labour,
Three men are discussing old wine.

Here a man broadcasts tips from the City
Through mouthfuls of savoury tart;
There a girl, quite heartbreakingly pretty,
Is grittily breaking a heart.

A couple holds hands between courses;
Their companions observe it with pain –
But they've splashed out on all the right horses,
And now they splash out on champagne.

The sea bass is praised, and the salmon,
And so is the great atmosphere;
Late arrivals, one rare steak, one gammon,
And bookings for twelve at New Year.

A liqueur with dessert? (Splendid fellow –
Lets no opportunity pass!)
And the chef, now amazingly mellow,
Accepts compliments, and a glass.

JOURNEY THROUGH MALDEN RUSHETT

The morning tingles, is singing in sunshine and frost.
Cold shadows shiver on pavements, linger on cars
On the dark side of the square, awaiting the sun.
I drive off to find you, chilly hands holding the wheel,
Intoxicated, perhaps, by the dry sparkling air,
But slowly, in nose to tail traffic along the King's Road
As always vibrating with zest, with its passion for life.
I dodge past a ponderous bus, brighter scarlet today,
Pass the town hall and its clock and turn left for the bridge,
A glittering joy to behold, its extravagant lace
Coruscating with frost in each curlicue.
The roadway is treacherous, black. As I reach the high point
The sun like a tiger from ambush leaps straight at my face,
Meets me eye to shocked eye, a golden and beautiful terror.
I slam on brakes, fumbling for sunglasses, dusty and cold,
Left over from summer. Now yet more alert, better armed,
I enter a gloomy defile, my back turned to the park,
Edging through dangerous shadows, slow motion. The sun
Turned rebel leader, deploying whole bands of insurgents,
Dazzles from well-chosen windows and snipes down the side-
                                                    streets,
Testing my defences: I go cautiously, shading my eyes,
On and around and through Wandsworth, leaving a space
For great , gleaming horses, ramming their way through the vans
Outside the brewery. Traffic is dead slow, then flowing
Down Putney Vale (ice barely skin deep, grasses frozen,
Air double-distilled.) Here I am well on my way
And the road is wide open –
                            – Time for judgment and skill
And pleasure in self-contained speed, on the lookout for snags.
Icy patch, slithering cars. That magician, the sun, reappears
Once again with his minions, in yet another disguise –

Paparazzi chasing a story, bulbs flashing from windscreens:
They circle the roundabout – flash – flash – flash – and zoom
away.
Chessington World of Adventures is clearly signed Closed.
(No adventures allowed until Spring? Seems too long to wait.)
Soberly through Malden Rushett – and into a dream:
A sprinkling of snow on the hill. The low sun
Burns like a bonfire, dark orange, melting the frost
Into gusts of billowing mist, smoke without scent;
And the trees – oh, the trees to either side of the road
Are either enchantment made real, a fairytale wood,
Or a fabulous stage-set quite rightly expecting applause.
Neither Lilac nor Sugar Plum Fairy, no sign of a Prince:
Just the delicate arching of branches, the brilliance of light,
The pale, arctic sky, the scenery all white and black
And, consciously elegant, two magpies, artfully placed.
So at the end of my journey I come to your door
As the light of this bright day is lifting into a sky
Barbaric, clear green, translucent behind the dark trees,
My mind full of magic, of Malden Rushett transformed,
An ethereal, otherworld kingdom of sunshine and frost.

Postcard from Thessalonica

The Meteora monasteries perched high,
Out of the world, to pray in peace for our sin;
A golden eagle planed higher, far up in the sky,
And saw the procession of tourist buses roll in.

WINNER TAKES ALL

He flaunts expensive jewellery, a tan,
Perfect white teeth, an intricate tattoo,
And calls out to the waiter, man to man,
'A bottle of the good stuff! Make that two!'

As the restaurant fills, his voice is raised –
He likes to feel he dominates the scene,
That others are both envious and amazed
To hear what he has done, and where he's been.

Seated at the table with his friends,
A smiling girl plays consort to his king;
Wherever her allegiance starts and ends
There's nothing rough about the diamond in her ring.

DESIGNATED DRIVER

Friends and relations react with alarm,
Or sometimes – not often – respect.
They say, 'Come on, a small glass will do her no harm
And can have very little effect.'

The truth is, she is as fond of a drink
As relations and friends mostly are,
But it's not the great sacrifice they seem to think –
She loves driving home in the car.

She savours a world given over to night,
Awake and alert. The locked park.
Unpredictable drivers. Fox caught in the light.
Empty roads, winding home in the dark.

DANDELION SUN

WHITE HORSES

White horse tossing playful manes,
    The breeze
Whisking morning mists away;
    Bright seas.
Mooring ropes cast neatly off –
    Job done;
Sails set, the seawall sliding aft;
    Warm sun.
Water chuckling low about
    Its own affairs;
Alive, the wheel talks to the hand;
    No cares.
Horizon wide as sky is high,
    As day is long;
Heart lifts and spreads its wings, and sings
    Its secret song.

WILD GEESE

Unwinding long skeins out of the morning light
They spend the bright day tamely grazing the meadows,
Domestic, orderly cattle: until the light fades,
Until colours merge, drain away down the lie of the land . . .
Abruptly, all at once run barking mad
They hurl their wild legions yelping into the wind
To stream headlong and reckless across the precipitous sky.
A dangerous pack in full cry, giving furious tongue,
They go hounding the pale, wily moon through gale-shredded
                                     clouds,
Until it soars, silent and scatheless – and out of their reach.

DIVING FROM THE BOAT

Toes gripping for extra stability, balance, a breath –
And swing forward into the dive, angled into warm seas
Cooler by blessed degrees than your sun-ripened skin,
The surface seamlessly parting, closing for you.
For just the count of a heartbeat, only for you,
Gravity loses all power, is at your fingers' ends.
Your curve through thin air continues unbroken through water
So clear you can see little shells on ribbed sands far below,
Bright fishes in spirals and shoals, graceful ribbons of weed,
The anchor-chain, silver, mysterious, stretching away,
Reaching up after invisible worlds overhead;
Moments as close to perfection as mortals can come,
With the secret sea murmuring music into your ear.

MYLOR

Wide, tidal river, smooth rush, slap and swirl –
The boat tugs its tether, fretting to be gone,
But here, a few yards from the sloping bank,
The looked-for miracle of fresh, clear water,
A place to stay, to preach, and work, and pray,
A well to make, cupping the precious spring.
Mylor climbed ashore and raised his hands.
After long nights and days of tossing waves,
No doubt the soft grass lurched beneath his feet
As his church floor tilts, swaying, under mine,
After more than sixteen hundred years.
His lasting legacy, a faithful flock. Wild flowers
Still cluster near the overflowing stream.

MIDSUMMER MOON

The moon, moving fast, has its spinnaker flying tonight;
It is racing its shadow, far out beyond Venus and Mars,
Taut orange canvas aglow and the sheets hauled in tight,
A weather-eye open for hazards, cloud-islands and stars.

A packet of chunky Crab sandwiches washed down with beer,
And the moon is in holiday mood, though night will not last long;
A neat gybe by the Pleiades and, as there's no one to hear,
The moon bellows snatches of tuneless, exuberant song.

Avoiding the shooting stars, comets and meteor showers,
It holds course through space, then turns back to where harbour
                                        lights burn,
Making the most of its few uninhibited hours;
And its wake, sparkling bright phosphorescence, curves
                                        sweetly astern.

The Fish leap like dolphins, upsetting the balancing Scales,
The Ram and the Bull raise their heads. Twins and Archer at
                                        play
Stare enviously as the moon creams past, trimming its sails –
Until the tide turns, and the dark begins ebbing away.

SUMMER SAILING

All day, each long day under the laughing sun
Islands and mountains dance about the blue,
Advancing and slipping sideways, heads held high,
Sidelong and backwards, swirling wooded slopes
With a white glimpse of rocky petticoats.
Dropping our anchor in some sheltered bay
We still their rush and movement and our own
Hold all the islands on a single chain;
Yet each night, all night, under the drifting moon,
Over the scented shore and silken sea,
Low in the tender sky, the twirling stars
Like fireflies dance on about the mast.

NO TIME, NO PLACE

There is no time, there is no place,
No sun, no moon, no stars, no space:
Dense mist lies on the water's face.

An almost silence. Any sound
Is muffled, muted, almost drowned:
Bird-calls, ripples lapping round.

No north, no south. No course to keep;
No need to sigh, or laugh, or weep;
The senses seem lulled half to sleep.

Until winds sweep the mists away,
The world hangs, small and pearly grey,
Suspended between night and day.

SWEETER THAN MAYBE

My heart may be able to sing, but is secret and shy;
My feet, though they're tempted to dance, are too timid to try;
My fingers may dream of a harp, or a wild violin,
But I rarely see gypsies,
Don't meet many angels –
I simply don't know where to start, and don't dare to begin.

If I heard of an angel or two with some moments to spare,
Or some really reliable gypsies with insights to share,
I could call on them when they flew in, or had space by their fires;
My hands could make music,
My songs pluck at heartstrings,
My dancing feet follow the tune as the rhythm requires.

Perhaps you would call, if an angel – or gipsy – agrees?
But not now. Now, my boat spreads its wings to the beckoning
breeze
In time to ride out with the tide, gliding swift as I please;
Life is sweeter than maybe
This luminous day
As I sail through the bay, and beyond, to the vagabond seas.

POSTCARD from Yarmouth

I love to watch a good storm,
And enjoy being out in a gale,
Provided my clothing is warm –
But never if we're under sail.

THE RACE

The yachts, closely spaced, heel over rounding the mark,
Elegant, streamlined, designed for both beauty and speed.
To the man on the golf course, a picturesque, colourful sight,
A challenge for the photographer down on the beach.
The naturalist think of a large pod of dolphins at play,
Or hunting together for food, like sea-wolves, in a pack.
The trained eye, here on the platform or further offshore,
Sees a ruthless, fiercely fought contest of courage and skill.
The weather stays neutral, whatever the windspeed, the rain,
And the sea owes no one allegiance, is both friend and foe.
The pampered, manicured boats are brutally tested,
Helm and crew, wasting few words, move swiftly as one,
Digging deep to give more of their best, then deeper again.
No quarter is given or asked, least of all for themselves.
This is no game, no idle day out on the water
Enjoying the scenery. No picnic: this is a race.

SEASIDE IDYLL

He lies back in his deckchair like a log,
Unwilling to be distracted from his book,
And says the kids are quite safe with the dog;
Sunning herself, she lifts her head to look.

Castles and quarrels, grit in someone's eye;
Splashes in shallow water, joyful screams;
At the ninth attempt, a fabulous sand-pie –
And can we have some money for ice-creams?

The dog slips off as sun cream's smoothed on backs
To gallop blissfully along the beach,
Where huge gulls swoop at him in feigned attacks,
Carefully gauged to stay beyond his reach.

He leaps high in the air, jaws open wide
In mock aggression, joining in the game,
And barks defiance at the incoming tide;
Then hurtles back, full pelt, when they call his name.

Sausages and pork pies, hard-boiled eggs,
Tomatoes and cold drinks; apples and gingerbread.
Fresh water for the dog. Sun cream on arms and legs,
Another swim; then time for home and bed.

OFFSHORE

'Winds light to moderate. Sea slight. Barometer steady.'

Midnight-blue water under fierce mid-morning sun;
White foam where the bow drives a path through the unheeding sea;
Wake rushing back, reaching out to the lands left behind.
Blinding bright diamonds, bright sapphires sparkle and wink
As the light ricochets from a myriad twinkling ripples;
A pale blue-grey sky veils invisible, distant horizons.
A wide world of emptiness but for our boat far offshore,
And an occasional elegant, wandering bird
Seen sweeping past with that effortless tilt of the wing,
Punctuating the blue and white scroll of the day
With scattered, random apostrophes, dashes and dots.

MOMENTS IN THE SOLENT

On a summer's day we sailed away
In bright and pleasant weather;
The crew learned lots of useful knots
And scrubbed the decks together,
And the Captain said: "I'm pleased to see all this effort and
devotion,
If you keep it up for a day or two, you may very well get
promotion."

This raised great hopes, and the crew coiled ropes,
(Their motto was Perfection),
Kept a good look-out, and learned to shout
When other ships changed direction.
We met with friends in foreign ports and partied without stopping;
Then the Captain said: "Shore leave till late", so everyone rushed off
shopping.

We had a great feast, twice a day at least,
And we kept our vessel tidy;
The Isle of Wight was our delight
But we had to be home by Friday.
Now we hadn't threaded the Needles yet, and wished we could
stay longer,
But the Captain said: "Life jackets on! The wind is getting stronger."

We got under way at the break of day
With all the moored boats jigging;
As we shot from the South through the harbour mouth,
The wind howled in their rigging;
And some of us were quite concerned and some of us felt queasy,
But the Captain said: "Get the foresail out", and then it all seemed
easy.

With wind and tide both on our side,
Heaven's answer to our wishes,
We flew along with a merry song
And our speed amazed the fishes.
Now some of us had blistered palms and some of us felt sick,
But the Captain said: "Trim the port backstay", and that seemed to
do the trick.

The food was all gone but for one stale scone,
Some cheese and a handful of raisins –
And a whacking great jar of the best caviar,
Kept hidden for these occasions.
Then the Captain chose a promising wave and surfed over
Chichester Bar,
And we berthed the boat, but still seemed to float, all the way home
in the car.

DANDELION SUN

Under a dandelion sun
Adrift in the rippling sky
Slides our silent boat; in the world afloat
Not a soul but you and I.

White dragon sea-foam rushes out
From the mouths of shadowed caves;
The frisky islands skip like goats
On the broad slopes of the waves.

Nosing their way, the smaller craft
Follow their hidden trails:
A hungry wind with folded wings
Stoops upon beating sails.

The horizon, tethered to our mast,
At once controlled and free,
Runs and wheels and counterspins
At the limits of the sea.

All across the smoothly polished glass
Of bright, translucent blue,
Not a sound is heard, not a beast, not a bird,
Not a soul but me and you.

Postcard from Doubtful Sound, New Zealand

Vertical waterfalls white as milk
Fall foaming over the cliff's rough face –
Yet, meeting a surface like dark green silk
They vanish, and leave neither stain nor trace.

MARINA

Shrieking their grief, a thousand bare-masted yachts,
Warped and shackled to walkways, all freedom gone,
Howl fury and heartbreak into the cutting, grey winds.
Last summer, each someone's darling, flattered, caressed
By warm waves and breezes, lovingly called by their names –
Butterfly – Nutmeg – Sweet Melody – Fleur – Northern Star –
Polished and petted, they sailed through the seas like proud swans,
Silent except for the singing of broad, silver wings.
Birds dipped in salute, suns rose up early to smile on them,
Dolphins and bright-scaled fish welcomed them into deep waters.
Nights smelled of spices and moonlight, of damp towels and gin,
Sounded with voices and music in quiet little bays.
Days galloped their way past like racehorses, eager and strong.
Tethered now, stripped and abandoned in numberless ranks,
Nameless and friendless, they rail at the uncaring sky,
Their taut shrouds keening a loudly discordant crescendo
Of frenzied resentment, of impotent, bitter complaint.

PELICAN BY THE SEA

By the sea, the pelican broods in his drab brown jacket
And gazes unblinking into the limpid water,
Long-faced and morose, ignoring the glittering small-fry.
His wide, flat feet are encased in yellow galoshes,
But his bald old cranium seems not to merit a sun hat.
Perfectly prehistoric, he sits there, unmoving,
Then suddenly lunges forward, a half-closed umbrella,
Snatching the paper bag containing his lunch
Before it is carried away by the wind and the water:
And returns to his post, shoulders hunched, giving nothing away.

PELICAN IN THE AIR

In the air, the pelican, footloose, no weight on his mind,
Glides like a barge under sail out along thermal currents
With effortless expertise, and with barely a glance,
Flaps only briefly and rarely when altering course.
He picks his way through the masts of the yachts at their moorings,
The broad wings, curved to a nicety, trimmed to the breeze,
Painted bright green from below by the sun off the sea.
Such a good morning for drifting alone in the blue,
Unhurried and happy, enjoying the taste of the day.
No great rush even to start on the business of fishing,
Though sooner or later he'll choose where to drop in to eat.

WADERS

It's hard to be keen about waders:
Hard to tell one from another.
They all have long legs bending backwards
And are not strongly coloured in winter,
And I can't tell my greenshanks from redshanks.
They wear pessimistic expressions
And hunch their long-suffering shoulders
Like mine, in the wind on the mudflats.
In this bitter weather, it's madness,
Or, anyway, only for birdbrains,
Coming to look at a curlew
Or a godwit, black-tailed or bar-tailed.
In a suitably glum illustration,
A dunlin is shown in the handbook
To be the most boring of waders.
But the incoming tide brings surprises;

Tame and tumbling and numberless,
In rolling flocks, close to the water,
With tender-eyed, kind little faces
Softly conversing together,
They sweep over and round us and past us
In a warm snowstorm of feathers,
Light and dark, turning and twisting:
An exhilaration of dunlins.

EAST THE WATER

There I stood, on Vinegar Hill,
East the Water, and longing to roam;
And for all I know, my shade stands there still,
Dreaming of freedom, wind and foam.

Away I went, in the howling gales,
When the timbers crack and it's wet and cold,
And icicles hang from the frozen sails,
And the setting suns turn the seas to gold.

Across the river and west away
To the ocean's edge and back again,
Where the naughty mermaids frisk and play,
Under burning heat and tropic rain.

Now, riding the rollers wild and grand,
Here am I, high on the swaying mast,
And I hope to be first with the shout of 'Land!'
And the sight of Vinegar Hill at last.

CORMORANT

Poised on a post, in arrogant display,
Half bird, half serpent: an heraldic beast,
Sable on argent rippled river water,
The neck, bend sinister. Fantastic, fit
To figure in some ancient bestiary,
An unlikely link in evolution's chain,
As if, emerging from primeval deeps,
A creature grew wings, took flight – against the rules,
Omitting the customary halfway stage,
The millennia crawling round some muddy swamp,
Considering options. Straight from sea to sky,
Riding the air in easy mastery,
Or buoyed by the current; plunging back down to feed,
Unheeding, at home in all three elements.
Aloof and ugly. Scaly, reptilian legs.
Dark angel's wings. Then, elegant, it dives –
Not to emerge until one thinks it drowned.

HERON

That tall, bony figure precise and impeccably dressed,
Is the senior partner of Herons. No wonder heads turn.
Austere though he looks, he is dangerous, greedy and sharp;
He commands, unsurprisingly, instant respect at the bank.
Patient and quite without sentiment in his affairs,
Deadly and accurate when he moves in for the kill,
He is known and feared for his ruthlessness and his long reach.
One can't guess his age or his interests, apart from his business.
Has he a family? (Strange thought!) A circle of friends?
Perhaps a dry sense of humour, carefully concealed?
Aloof and unsmiling, apparently quite self-contained,
Long neck doubled back, he sails impassively past.

ON THE MUDFLATS

Oystercatcher,

Oystercatcher;

One-note peeper,

Banish sleeper,

Urgent crier,

Speedy flier,

Snappy dresser,

Onward presser,

What's your worry?

Why the hurry?

Ahoy, my hearty!

Where's the party?

Winging on,

Already gone,

Spotlight snatcher

Oystercatcher.

THE ANCHORAGE

Another dazzling day shines to a close,
The sun, that early riser, swiftly sets,
Translucent twilight deepens to dusk and dark.
Voices are stilled. Breeze drops, and silver strings
Finish their pizzicato on the masts.
The boat creaks, content and weary, safe at rest
After the strong wind's pull, the foaming rush,
Shouted commands, the fiercely eager sails.
The anchor-chain snores softly at the bow;
The sea breathes regularly, half asleep,
Lulling, soothing, hushing the whispering shingle.
When a big ship passes, far offshore,
The beat of its great heart sounds below decks,
Dwindling into distance and into silence.

NIGHT WATCH

Suspended far above human concerns,
Aloof – uncaring – remote –
When daylight fades, a moon-lamp burns,
And is greeted as if a friend returns,
A companion, a guide, as the wide world turns,
Lighting a path for our boat.

A different moon, night after night,
Appears at the ocean's rim,
Pale and small or large and bright,
Soaring each to its chosen height,
Sometimes reluctant to quench its light
When planets and stars grow dim.

One is slender and sharp, curved like a blade,
Perhaps hunting for lion or bear;
One round and ripe for a bombing raid,
Or a midnight feast, or illicit trade;
Once a listening ear, bizarrely mislaid,
Hung in the wondering air.

And one moonrise looked like a ship on fire,
Deceiving the startled eye;
Like a northern chieftain's funeral pyre,
Orange and gold to amaze and inspire;
The brilliant blaze burned fiercely higher
Till the moon took to the sky.

But tonight no sign of a moon at all –
No light, no comfort, no mark,
The sky just a stifling purple pall,
And, driving blindly into a wall
Of inky blackness and coming squall,
Goes our lonely boat in the dark.

POSTCARD from Poole

Hordes of sunburned tourists were seen
Where the lifeboat moored alongside the quay;
Cool, slender Jenny in blue and green
Waved and was gone, like a breeze off the sea.

SPLICE THE MAINBRACE !

Fair-weather sailor, old salt, bailer,
Houseboat, narrow boat, speedboat, yacht.
Helmsman, grinder, don't leave me behinder,
Navigator, deckhand. *Give it all you've got.*
Fresh air, set fair, don't care, au pair,
Down in the galley there, mind you watch the pot.
Barnacle scraper, stand around and gaper,
There's whisky in the bottle, let's have another tot.
Shooting star, Jack Tar, floating spar. *Going far?*
Diver, survivor, rain and rust and rot.
Reef that mainsail, here comes another gale.
Was that a blue whale? Tie a firmer knot!
Lighthouse keeper, never fall asleeper,
Hope the water's deeper in this very rocky spot.
Dicing with disaster, past the harbourmaster,
Other boats aghast – and that's about the lot.

BECALMED

Becalmed. The coast a hundred miles away.
A lazy swell lifts and rocks the boat.
No breeze, no breaking waves. For half a day
No change. No birds. No other ships afloat.

Lulled and soothed by constant, gentle motion,
We struggle to stay alert. Watch must be kept.
Huge tankers or other monsters of the ocean
Might overwhelm us, unseen, if we slept.

The day is ending, darkness coming on.
Distance means nothing. We confront our fears.
The boat rocks. The horizon now is gone
And all sense of direction disappears.

Calm sea. No cloud. No man-made source of light.
A young moon in a sky filled to the brim
With crowding stars, yellows, pinks, blues and white –
And danger itself, eclipsed, appears to dim.

Jupiter hangs like the jewel an emperor craves.
The stars are steady in the arching sky.
Reflected stars move gently with the waves –
Or could be the lights of shipping passing by.

In a globe of stars, snatched up without trace,
For spellbound hours we float in the Milky Way,
Helpless, enchanted, outside time and space,
Awestruck, bedazzled – yet longing for the day.

THE LADIES OF THE THAMES

Knightsbridge is, of course, at their feet;
Rhine-maidens just can't compete –
but they set off and sail through the ghastliest gale,
and their hearts do not quail and their nerves do not fail,
for they're Ladies of The Thames.

Afloat in a boat they scoff at all dangers;
ashore, what is more, they are flower arrangers,
dog handlers, sportswomen, intrepid riders –
some of them aren't afraid even of spiders,
these brave Ladies of The Thames.

They are potters and painters and autograph signers,
art dealers, silversmiths, garden designers,
quibblers and nibblers and scribblers of verses,
and ballet dancers, lawyers and nurses,
all Ladies of The Thames.

Philosophy students and cordon bleu cooks,
and computer tutors and writers of books;
Some are said to be wilful – shall we say one in ten? –
but all of them skilful leaders of men –
Ladies, I give you –
The Ladies of The Thames.

ANZAC DAY DINNER

A TOAST

However fine the spoken words
Or sweetly played the song,
They were sent by distant overlords
Whose strategy was wrong.

However high the memorial stone,
Or beautifully said
Tributes of praise for them alone,
Thousands of men fell dead.

Some few came back, and taught us how
Remembrances to keep:
Prayers have been prayed, tears shed, but now,
In their memory, drink deep.

VOYAGE Of DISCOVERY

PORT GRIMAUD

A peaceful night. Time to let in the day.
Early sunlight skips across rippling water,
Gleaming and glinting, playing ducks and drakes.
Quiet sounds of splashing. Loud, vibrant engine noise –
A boat casts off from a neighbouring garden's end,
Slipping away towards the open sea.
Reflected colours, wavering in its wake,
Are houses, shutters, terracotta tiles,
Two bright, forgotten towels, left out to dry.
A morning full of promise, already warm;
The smell of fresh coffee floats up from below.
A bird's-eye view of hedges along the canal,
The taller shrubs moving gently in the breeze –
Reds, greens, two blues, a silver and a mauve,
White and yellow, tangerine and cream,
And more than six or seven shades of pink:
Rose, salmon, apple-blossom, bitter-almond, peach . . .

SIENA

Far above ancient, noble roofs they fly,
The screeching swifts, graphite on slate-blue sky.
They trace rapid hieroglyphs I cannot read,
Write and erase themselves at breakneck speed,
And, whirling, soaring, tumbling as they snatch
Their unseen prey, exultant, on the catch,
Inscribe mysterious histories, not intended
Ever to be caught or comprehended.

HILLTOP VILLAGE

Steep, climbing, flower-hung streets between stone walls and houses,
wander and intertwine, turn themselves into steps,
join forces and separate. Each one leads up to the church,
discovered at length, triumphantly crowning the hill.
Bougainvillea and roses tumble and sprawl,
the air smells of water, damp leaves and wet earth;
outside the shop, of coffee and freshly baked bread,
inside, of onions and oranges, spices and soap.
Customers, suitably greeted as they enter and leave,
in dialect or lingua franca, exchange nods and smiles.
This balcony, for a brief spell, is the hub of the place,
overlooking the small square, observing its comings and goings
and partly screened by the fig tree casting its shade.
Bottles rattling in crates, bustle, whistling and gossip;
and the solos and chorus of the morning's ritual dance
have as their backdrop the windows, the cobbles, the pots,
the streets slipping off to the main road, the shapes of the landscape.
Then doors close. Shade, passersby melt away,
leaving the sun to burn fiercely, assuming control –
until the horizon swings upwards and cool evening comes.

PAESTUM

Whoever the first owner was,
Now several gods swear: "It's mine!"
It's a bone of contention, because
The building's remarkably fine –
So this may be the temple of Zeus
Or Poseidon, or some other one;
But let scholars – and gods – call a truce
At the going down of the sun.

As evening shades into night,
A haze turns the sky milky pale,
And a single planet hangs bright
Over a home-going sail;
Whether Venus – or possibly Mars –
I really won't venture to say.
Those twinkling clusters of stars
Are the fishing boats out in the bay . . .

But one planet has now become four,
Crowding jealously on to the stage,
Illuminating the shore
With truly incandescent rage,
And fiercely pressing the claim
That the temple is rightfully theirs.

Ye gods! Have you no sense of shame
In your endlessly wrangling affairs?
I have travelled some way to enjoy
This place. Since you cannot agree,
Kindly pack yourselves off back to Troy,
And leave lovely Paestum to me.

CHESS TOURNAMENT

The White Queen is poised in readiness for the fight,
Impassive counsellors on either hand.
Her soldiers' scimitars glint sharp and bright,
And, on her hills, strong towers defend the land.

Rich silks, rare jewels proclaim her power, her money;
That legendary face, mysterious eyes,
The ivory skin, the voice as sweet as honey,
Conceal a cold and ruthless enterprise.

The Red ranks are sailors, armed for war; their Queen
Floats on the waves, like one of Venus' daughters,
Lovely to look at, graceful and serene,
Her marble palaces kissed by the waters.

Her ministers are cunning, and adept
At use of poisons, stabbings in the back.
They point with pride to great bronze horses, kept
As trophies from an unprovoked attack.

Action commences. Pawns are sacrificed
In defence of precious trade routes to the East,
Ambassadors sent out, new friends enticed,
The greater losses weighed against the least.

Byzantium, Venice, equal in power and fame,
Their wealth, their strength, their beauty, closely matched;
This constant, deadly struggle is no game –
Each wants the other crushed, brought down, despatched.

So it continues. Gaining or losing ground,
Defeats are suffered, fortunes are restored;
Then, far to the West, a rich new world is found:
The mocking gods have overturned the board.

POSTCARD from Slinfold

In your own deceptively simple style,
Whatever the challenges at the start,
With decision, taste and no little guile,
You make of each house a work of art.

ISTANBUL

All along roadside verges, surprisingly green in the heat,
carpets of well-watered grass, arabesques of bright flowers;
under shady trees in the parks, coffee kiosks and chairs.
Huge flags here and there, splashes of scarlet and gold,
mark places of legend: Topkaki, Hagia Sofia.
Traffic spins past Roman walls, then is slowed to a crawl –
in the ancient mazes of streets the pedestrian is king.
Fierce sun blazes down on the harbour's glittering waters,
on towering cruise ships moored alongside busy quays.
Ferries speed madly about, discordantly honking like geese.
Stationed on Galata Bridge, cheerful fishermen reel in their catch
while eager fish, thronging below, fling themselves on to hooks.
Everywhere, mosques in all sizes, modest or grandly ornate.
Markets, both outdoors and under vast acres of roof,
sell gold, copper, Turkish Delight – in too many flavours to count –
vividly coloured spices in pungent, conical heaps,
carpets, leather jackets and coffee pots, saffron and shoes.
At sunset, a breeze fans the rosy face of the Bosphorus,
and the call to prayer rings out from tall minarets,
startling the birds. An immense flock flies up in alarm,
seabirds and pigeons together in a whirling tornado,
circling and soaring, wings caught in the mellowing light.

MOUNT ATHOS AT SUNRISE

Up glides the sun behind veils of mist low on the water;
The translucent sky is tenderest mother of pearl,
The sea so vivid a red it is staining our ship.
The holy mountain, colossal, triangular, black,
And more than a mile high, rears up straight out of the waves,
Still robed and hooded in darkness, hands tucked in its sleeves.
It wears a lop-sided halo of wavering cloud,
Nudged slightly askew, unheeded, as of no account.
Beyond, the strengthening light shows the dangerous coast,
Precipitous cliffs overhung by minute hermit cells,
Woods, scattered meadows, grand monasteries, rocky bays.
A harshly beautiful world, set apart, out of time –
Paradise so they say, but with all its gates firmly barred.
Respectfully, we keep our distance, then put back out to sea.

RETURN TO LEPTIS MAGNA

Long streets, long remembered, stretch away in the sun,
Empty, paved in marble, and white as long ago;
Pillars stand re-erected, of every thousand, one –
Tokens of past magnificence. Strong, cooling breezes blow.
Infinitely peaceful; and soothing to hear once more
Sea-surge, singing its way towards the shore.
                                        – space –
Museum-worthy, the statues have jostled their way to town;
Alone in the noble ruins, Medusa keeps her place.
Great theatre, markets, unpeopled. No ships cast their anchors down.
No sad city, for all that. Here the bright years, spinning
Almost unnoticed, pause: and wind back to their beginning.

AT WENGEN STATION

A palette almost entirely black and white
Barely suggests some colour here and there –
The cream of sheer rock-faces shadowed brown,
A faint wash of green about far conifers
Clambering darkly to the sunlit alp.
Close to the shining rails, at centre stage,
Painted with light and air, the leafless tree
Outlined against the snowy mountainside
Welcomes a restless, whistling band of choughs;
They flutter merrily from branch to branch,
Pecking at clusters of last season's seeds.
An artist might omit the power lines,
The arriving, gleaming-yellow clockwork train,
The cheerful passengers, bright clothes and skis.
But now the train moves out. The birds have flown.
The tree is just an ordinary tree.

BAIT AL SAHIL

A modest house. A most stupendous view
from its height above the sandy little bay
over the glorious sea. Flowering shrubs in pots.
The splashing of a fountain to cool the air.
Once, an acquaintance, early in the day,
(harnessed, it turned out, to a power-boat
invisible behind the rocks below)
mysteriously floated in mid-air.
Once, an osprey, fishing. Once, a fighter jet
climbing as it cleared the low terrace wall . . .
Each evening, a golden egg-yolk sun,
serenely swallowed by the waiting waters.

LADY IN FURS

On to the little train she grandly swept –
Heady scent and husband trailed behind –
And settled, as if extra space were kept
For her alone, no question in her mind.

We passengers, unless deaf, were allowed
To hear incisive comments she might pass;
Her voice, being confident and rather loud,
Etched trite opinions on the toughened glass.

The scenic journey was, it seemed, destroyed.
If I were to feel comfortable again,
Rather than sit there, ruffled and annoyed,
I would do well to move along the train.

And then my eye fell on her little foot,
So exquisitely shaped, softly caressed
By its elegantly hand-stitched little boot;
I smiled, and quite forgave her all the rest.

POSTCARD to the Potter

*Your imprint on your work is such
That, as I prepare and serve a meal,
Each well-shaped bowl speaks of your touch,
Your clever hands, the turning wheel.*

ON THE BEACH AT ANZAC COVE

They are not forgotten, though time goes by –
We come to salute, in sorrow and pride,
Those who were here, those heroic men,
Our kin and their comrades, who fought and died.

Sinners and saints and farmers and clerks,
These were real men, with their lives to live,
Tough, self-reliant and obstinate –
So much to lose. So much to give.

Grasping for victory out of reach,
Facing an enemy, fierce and brave,
They hurled themselves upwards at the cliffs,
Were broken, fell back, like a breaking wave.

In the heat and cold, in the wind and rain,
Far from the lands where they were born,
They defied overwhelming odds, and fell,
Cut down like poppies in the corn.

PANORMOS

A perfect harbour, sheltered on every side,
with no one anchoring except ourselves.
Faint, tinkling goat-bells. Peace . . . but for the wasps
which droned annoyingly about the boat
till darkness fell. A glass of wine, a meal,
an idyllic moonlight swim, a quiet night . . .
But at earliest daybreak, ready and armed for war,
in close formation, whole squadrons of wasps were there.
They drove us from our mooring out to sea,
and harried and pursued us far from shore.

MOONSTRUCK

Above the silent peaks the moon rides high,
Brilliant beyond belief, in a cloudless sky
Studded with vibrant constellations. Each
Separate star hangs almost within reach.
Impossible to sleep away the night.
The mountain snows gleam with surreal light,
Clear as the day, with no reflecting glare.
Shutters are closed. The village streets are bare;
Meadows are smooth as freshly laundered beds;
Chairlifts and cabins roost inside their sheds.
Time is suspended, vanquished, and the dark
Reduced to snipped-out silhouettes: black, stark,
Mysterious shadows, serried ranks of trees.
The still air kills with cold. Warm blood will freeze,
Timber, metal, stone will split and break.
The church clock, keeping faith with those awake,
Measures eternity with its quiet bell;
And still the bright moon casts its unearthly spell.
Aloof, aggressive, searching out hidden spies,
It shoots silver bullets, wounding unwary eyes,
While, glacier-slow, it drifts the whole night long,
Until birds have begun their morning song.

MUSEUM PIECE, HERAKLION

Stopped in my tracks, entranced: the Phaistos Disc.
Above all else, a lovely artefact,
Fashioned with subtle skill from red-gold clay;
Merely a span across, and biscuit-thin,
Embossed with unknown symbols on each face.
Fragile, old, astoundingly intact –
And silent as once was the Rosetta Stone.
Unique. Were there perhaps a thousand more?
What is the message? Are these magic charms?
A tally of some sort – goods, horses, men?
Why circular in shape? Why spiralled signs?
From centre out or starting at the rim?
Pick your own theory and make it stick –
Or linger, like me, only to admire
An object of such cunning craftsmanship.

Contract:

Your wife, great prince, now places in your hand
Her hand, herself and everything she has.
Your honour is to her a sacred trust,
Her whole delight to please and comfort you.
Your life is more to her than life itself.
She swears this from her soul before the gods.

Your husband, lady, binds himself to you
With sacred oaths before the listening gods.
He will protect you, keep and honour you
And treasure you above all else he has.
If he should fall, be sure his shade will wait
Lonely for you upon the farther shore.

NORTHERN SUMMER

Land and sea float adrift in a summer dream.
Blackback hills. A ragged snowy crest.
Dolphin waves. The dove-pale ripples gleam
With the tender colours of a pigeon's breast.

Lazy hours to savour and to share,
Watercolour skies washed blue or grey,
Quicksilver fish, green grass and scented air
In the charmed circle of an endless day.

Light celebrates light. In honour of Saint John,
Fireworks and bonfires; no one will sleep tonight.
Free as a bird, the sun goes winging on,
Flaunting bright burnished feathers in its flight.

A thirsty swallow now, it starts to slide
Towards the water, kissing its chosen mark –
And swoops to begin its graceful upward glide,
Taunting the hungry grey wolf of the dark.

NEVER MIND THE LEMONS

Never mind the lemons, glowing yellow
On beds of ice, with strands of bladderwrack,
And plates of thinly-sliced brown bread and butter,
All set on a crisp, white, damask tablecloth.
Don't bother me with chopped shallots and vinegar;
No dash of red Tabasco is required.
We stand waist-deep in water, warm and clear,
Breaking the small, sweet oysters from the rocks,
Then carry them up the quiet, deserted beach:
Trophies to feast on, sitting side by side
On one bright-patterned towel. Moments of bliss
To take away for ever. Never mind the pearls.

CARIBBEAN BEACH

Little waves dance to a tropical beat,
White foam patterns the sand at my feet;
Water as clear as any I've seen,
Further offshore becomes aquamarine,
And further yet, where the ships glide through,
The sea is a deep and royal blue;
Farthest of all, too far to swim,
A silvery gleam marks the wide world's rim.
After sundown the day ends soon –
But then come the stars and the friendly moon.

CARIBBEAN SUNSET

Progressing with due pomp and circumstance down to the sea,
The sun sails away towards distant, more westerly lands.
Flowers, loyal subjects, cluster to watch him depart,
Relinquish their store of bright colours to splash on the sky
As a gorgeously outlandish banner with fringes of gold,
In bold streaks of crimson and scarlet, of orange and rose.
It waves bravely at the horizon: it fades: is gone.
The sea surface changes, absorbs turquoise into itself,
Deepens to indigo-blue. Brief glimpses of lace
Are white crests, surging forward and vanishing, surging again.
Large or small, boats and birds all steer a straight course for
                                                        home,
Glide shoreward, make landfall, and thankfully fold weary
                                                        wings.

OCEAN'S EDGE

The lush garden rings to a chorus of birds
Contrapuntally singing their song without words;
Warblers, bananaquits, grackles – and doves
Of smooth terracotta, bemoaning lost loves;
And hummingbirds busily working like bees,
Plundering sweetness from blossoming trees:
      Bougainvillea, jasmine, and gold alamanda,
      Hibiscus, poinsettia, blue jacaranda.

Ginger-plants show off sharp pinks, fiery reds,
Bird-of-paradise blooms raise cool, elegant heads;
Palms and mahogany reach for the sky,
Casuarinas grow feathers and fly;
Unquenchable shrubs flaunt leaves brilliant as flowers,
Resplendent in sunshine, ablaze in the showers:
      Bougainvillea, jasmine, and gold alamanda,
      Hibiscus, poinsettia, blue jacaranda.

And, changing and changeless, unfettered and free,
Restless and calm – always – always the sea;
      Always – always – always
      Always the sea.

Postcard from Oman:

Shuttered against the heat of the day,
Silent, deserted, a narrow street
With high blank walls giving nothing away;
Snippets of bright silks lay at my feet.

EUROMOS

A quiet valley, well outside the town
And full of olive trees; a hidden spring;
Morning light, and sunshine pouring down;
The grass grows thickly here, and small birds sing.

A pretty little temple, built for Zeus,
No larger than a modest village hall,
Thrown open to the winds. Long out of use,
Columns unroofed; no sanctuary at all.

No thunderbolts are feared, no omens seen;
Of statues, priests or worshippers, no trace.
Among the leaves, olives hang, green on green –
A heavy crop; a pleasant, fertile place.

But, after nightfall – then how might it be?
Without the panting bus, the patient guide:
Lonely, in moonlight, no one there but me,
The tumbled stones, and silence at my side.

WAITER

Descendent of fishermen on the beach
And peasant girls selling onions and fruit,
He can read and write, uses standard speech,
And goes to work in a neat blue suit.

His photograph is his mother's pride,
In a frame befitting the family star,
His pale face is an infallible guide
To full-time employment. He has come far.

SKYSCRAPER

I'm high as a kite on the altitude, the unexpected,
Carried away in mid-air Mid-America.
So please overlook it if I seem slightly above myself –
Eighty floors in a wink and a blink, in a twinkling
Wall-to-wall windows and the most stupendous of views.
White wine appears on a tray, a glass put in my hand
As we stand among flowers and books and deep leather chairs,
Strangely familiar surroundings, strangely located.
From up here I can see the wide world is a giant aquarium
Where creatures of all kinds live life on their several levels:
Planes soar and glide in the sky in the rarefied air,
While far, far below us, down there in the heavier heat,
Shinily carapaced cars crawl in orderly rows,
Following well-defined lines and rigidly ruled;
Boats, close beside them, have freely curving trajectories,
The chalk marks stretching behind them quickly erased.
People and birds seem at liberty, roaming at random . . .
Excuse me, I'm sorry? You spoke to me? Luncheon is served?
If you want me to think about food or to talk about business
It would have to be on a day the aquarium's closed –
All that movement and colour screened off behind curtains of
                                                    cloud.

HAMMERSHOI AT HOME

Patches of sunshine gilding wooden floors,
The piano in its place against the wall,
A passage-way between two open doors –
My brush defines and celebrates them all.
Light falling on your half-averted face,
A treasured bowl, a single, polished chair,
An ordered, peaceful calm. Quiet colours. Space.

Time flowing on, unthreatening. Time to spare.
Not for me upheavals, crowds and noise,
Discomfort, heat, harsh cries in alien lands.
This harmony I love, composure, poise,
The gestures of your busy, careful hands.
Challenging, simple subjects. I aspire
To paint the rainbow's end, my heart's desire.

VOYAGE OF DISCOVERY

Quietly casting its moorings, the house puts to sea;
the gardens slide smoothly astern, blown away by the breeze.
Seen from the library, dolphins frolic and glide
Where, this morning, deer cropped the roses. A journey begins
towards the faraway places of our hearts' desires,
in those countries where the sun rises, or where the sun sets,
or where night is bright as the day for a whole summer long.
Castles in Spain or Arabia, snow-covered peaks,
barren sands, steep rugged hillsides; fields of wild flowers
surrounding white temples and palaces; long flights of steps;
veiled women; hammocks and donkey-carts, camels, canoes . . .
Somebody plays jazz piano. Friends come and go
or sip drinks, reviewing the day and discussing tomorrow.
Life was never more real, never more like a dream,
as, in glimmering darkness, unhurried, the house travels on.

DESPATCH FROM ELSEWHERE

Not merely a new world. This is a different planet.
Great fiery suns blaze all across burning skies,
Cartwheeling widdershins. At night, unknown stars
Are suspended against dark blue velvet, like clusters of gems;
Some, reflecting our own constellations, are set upside down.
No dawn chorus, but a daily explosion, a terrible racket
From squabbling, screeching, bright-feathered, furious birds
With never a thought for their neighbours. A deep friendly voice
Can sometimes be heard, laughing merrily out in the woods.
Trees eat other trees. Fantastic creatures abound
In the violently coloured, harsh and unyielding landscapes
And vast tracts of untamed, challenging, unsettled country.
Heat, cold, wind, rain, drought, floods – all are extreme,
And apocalyptic fires rage out of control.
Great cities are widely spaced round the continent's rim:
Skyscrapers, airports, an utterly breath-taking harbour;
Domesticated acreage, farms, parks and gardens,
Vivid blue wrens, pink robins, and larks the size of a beetle.
Good beer, good wine, and abundant, wonderful food.
A place like no other. It forges its own kind of people.

WILDLIFE EXPERT

Some credit them with thoughts much like our own –
They gaze about them with that wondering frown
Trying, perhaps, to puzzle out the world,
Or turn small objects in their clever hands.
Almost they could be relatives of ours!
Though primitive, they're organised in groups
With certainly a formal hierarchy,
Amusing to watch when they don't know you're there.
They're mostly harmless, but don't go too near –
Though some respond to friendly overtures,
They are suspicious, easily alarmed –
And that means trouble. Also, I have found
You cannot trust those skulking on their own.
Sadly, they seem to be a dying breed –
I rarely see a female with its young –
But sometimes find in one troop several kinds.
These new ones, now – I've only seen the males –
They seem to need protection from the sun
And won't be parted from their sunglasses.

NIGHT MUSIC – frogs in concert

As day ends, night descends. Abruptly, when birds are gone,
Night music bursts forth without inhibition or pause.
Clear ringing calls fill the air as from numberless bells,
Flutes with only two notes try to outplay each other,
Amateur steel drummers go for it, hammer and tongs;
Carried away – but in desperate need of a leader –
It's a contest, rehearsal, performance all rolled into one.
Most flowers sleep. White blooms, awake in the dark,
Listen in silence, nodding their heads, gently swaying,
Or, entranced by cacophony, perfectly still.

MAPUTO

Noon bludgeons broad, shade-less avenues, the maze
Of corrugated roofs and alleyways,
Station, cathedral. Away from the sunbaked street
At the ocean's edge, a strong breeze soothes the heat.
Carvings, seashells, necklaces, change hands
At stalls, and on the roadway near the sands.
Bright cloths dance out from lines rigged up for sale.
A woman tips her cockle-laden pail
Into an empty sack, and digs for more,
Barefoot and barelegged, harvesting the shore.
Back from their fishing, twenty painted dhows
With sharply angled masts and upswept bows
Bob here at rest, antiquity afloat.
The glittering catch is landed from each boat
And promptly sold. The world heads home as soon
As the low sun sets; the end of afternoon.
Short twilight, sudden darkness. Now is heard
The grave and ritual chanting of a bird,
Haunting and lovely, in a minor key,
Floating out over the listening, sighing sea.

EARTH'S INFINITE VARIETY

Distance lends enchantment to the moon –
A dead rock, gilded with a borrowed glow;
It envies our green and blue world, night and noon,
Vibrant with life and colour, rush and flow –
Rivers and rainbows; fish, fruit, flowers and trees;
Oceans; and beasts, birds, butterflies and bees.

FLOWERS PLAY JAZZ
WEST AFRICAN POEMS

RAIN BEFORE DAWN

Rain falls at night, an hour before the dawn,
Blue skies, cool breezes – now the perfect days
Follow each other, strung on a silver chain,
Glowing with colour, rounded, reflecting light.
Busy canoes swoop past on tattered sails,
Leaves freshly dyed in every shade of green
Frame flitting birds in every patch of blue;
Flowers, dressed to kill, outdance the butterflies.
The days drift into evening, warm and clear;
Clouds, purple, lazy, float in a pale pink sky,
Kingfishers plunge in waters tinted rose –
And fresh rain falls, like blessings, before dawn.

LONG BEFORE LIGHT

Long before light, anticipating day,
Tired girls in daytime make-up, smart as paint,
Their faces still asleep, move through the dark –
Feet in high heels treading familiar pavements,
Pausing; sleep-walking through the grumbling cars
To wait at familiar bus stops. Young men in overalls,
Soldiers, policemen, sleepy market women,
Crowd into taxis next to city suits,
Briefcases, cufflinks. Truckloads of men
Packed in together, travel the roads to town,
Bumping and swaying, their drivers half awake.
Street lamps begin to fade. The waters gleam
Pale in the harbour. Birds perched on cables call,
Calling and calling for the dark to lift,
Insisting. Time for the coming of the light.

FISHING CANOES

Canoes slide past, grey on pale pearly gray,
Outside my wide windows in the early light,
Silent as tranquil dreams, not fast, not slow,
Going with the steady flowing tide.
Men sit to paddle, straddle with the net,
Paired darker grey against the watery gleam,
Poised and surefooted on the rocking shells,
Spellbound and noiseless. An arm uncoils in air –
Cobweb-light the round net spreads and falls.
Faultless and lovely, like ballet on high wires,
Untiring the dancers fish, the fishers dance,
In their primeval trance, in early light.

SUNRISE

Sun rouses himself, touches the master switch,
Instantly floods the world with a tide of colour.
Green runs along the trees, across the grass,
Cars, buildings, fences are silver, brown or blue.
Anonymous shapes become persons, each one unique,
Brightly or soberly, richly, flamboyantly dressed,
Or barefoot, bare-chested, torn trousers rolled to the knee.
Slogans on hoardings, butterflies, road signs and taxis
Leap into focus. And with the coloured tide, noise –
Doors, windows open, slam closed. Engines roar on the road.
The hooting, vibrating buses clamour for room.
The children giggle and chatter their way to school,
Head-balanced satchels shielding sun-dazzled eyes.
"Customer! Customer!" women urgently call,
"Tomatoes, lettuce, cucumber, I have sweet oranges!"

Under the trees at the roadside, passport photographers,
Hairdressers, people with brooms, in a tangle of languages
Greet and gossip and joke. Next to the drain,
A man hangs dyed cloths along the accustomed wall.
The sun has roused himself and the world together –
Life sings through all the wires of the wide-awake day.

GOSSIP COLUMN

Hustle and bustle, a typical newspaper office –
Here with the Village Weaver, life's one long mad rush,
a crisis, a fever, a frenzy, a race against time,
taxis, yellow and black, departing, arriving,
fresh material gathered and rushed to the scene,
urgent despatches flown in right up to the deadline,
miles of telexes, endless ribbons of paper –
the whole place swarming with colourful, volatile characters,
gossiping, posturing, all showing off to each other.
Squabbles flare up and are settled – there's work to be done
though the pecking order's a terribly sensitive issue.
None of them saints, of course, much as you might expect –
a quick drink now and then – a fellow has to keep going –
the occasional flutter, a skirmish or two on the side
and, don't even ask, all with an eye for the birds –
Life must go on, after all, so why not enjoy it?
And then, at the end of the day, after all that performance,
when all the loose ends are tied in and the job has been done,
what is there to show for all that crafting of articles,
the mixture of zest and compulsion, adrenalin, noise?

A million weaver birds' nests hung from one palm tree.
Even the fruit bats next door are impressed. Can't be bad.

THE ISLAND

Backs to the sun, gazing out over the water,
The fisher huts huddle their rough-thatched heads together,
Crowding companionably down to the edge of the shore,
Jostling and gossiping, telling old fishermen's tales –
But keeping a critical eye on the dipping of paddles,
Weighing the rhythm, the balance, the casting of nets,
Wise to the wind's shifts, watching each change in the weather
In the brown expanses of mirror reflecting the sky.
They choose to ignore the busy road hard on their heels,
Unheeding of traffic, the toxic fumes, grinding of gears,
And anything else that is less than a hundred years old.
In an orderly line near the harbour, some distance away,
Their skyscraper grandchildren stand, ambitiously tall,
Politely respectful, giving the ancestors room –
Discreetly keeping the present day screened from their sight.

THE GARDEN

From morning till evening the flowers play jazz in the sun
on unmuted trumpets, bright yellow, scarlet and peach,
orange and tangerine, loudly and blithely together
in honky-tonk harmonies, high on their own syncopation.
Saxophones moan indigo; electric guitars
pluck shocking pink chords and arpeggios of purple and mauve.
A vocalist, solo, is swinging and singing the blues.
Vibrant, the violins, rainbow-hued, crooning and sobbing,
tangle and blend with a double bass, crimson and puce,
and the pulsing, insistent percussion of red upon red.
All day they play to the green, to the swaying, ecstatic,
                              the hypnotised leaves.

MID AFTERNOON

Mid afternoon. It is hot. The road is deserted
But for the traders sitting well back in the shade,
And the man walking by with the sewing machine on his
                                                    shoulder.
A couple of watchmen saying long prayers by the gate –
Empty and quiet but for the lumbering buses,
Gentle mechanical tinkerings under a car,
A tired traffic warden thirstily cooling his throat
With oranges bought from the girl in the blue and red
                                                    wrapper,
Her sister giggling shyly and peeling the fruit.
The sun beats weightily down on a scene without people,
Apart from two lawyers carrying briefcases, wigs,
Crossing to stand in the usual place for a taxi,
Waving away the boy proffering peanuts and socks.
A gardener clips off long strands of pink-flowering creeper,
Singing in time with the rhythmical scratch of a rake.
No one about except two children chasing the chickens,
Disturbing the placid goats browsing along the white wall.
Their mother, baby on broad back, chats to her neighbours,
Women hanging out washing under the trees:
The road is quite empty and silent, abandoned to heat.

THE TREE

My own tree, feathered, fronded green,
Crowned overhead with vivid flowers
And hung about with orchid plants in pots,
My green tree, stretching kindly hands,
Its green sap rising, is alive with birds,

With hops and hoverings, with sudden flights,
Flutterings, flirtations and alarms –
Busy with darting sorties after flies,
Loud with clear mocking scales and raucous calls,
Melodic whistled notes and plaintive songs.
Sun dapples through the rustling foliage,
A wheeling falcon passes, curves away,
Small birds drift in flocks like wind-blown leaves.
A couple of tabby lizards on the trunk
Nod, head pointing up, head pointing down.
The tree laughs in its pleasure, bends and sways
As kingfisher rests and folds his magic cloak.

BIRDS

In the green morning garden, cool and still,
Birds in profusion, blending as many songs,
Weave their bright-feathered flights from tree to tree,
Cling to bending sprays in parties to feed,
Glide, stately and slow, dart like small arrows,
Restless, alert and free, swooping and calling,
Until the intemperate sun moves up the sky:
Spiderweb mists between tree trunks shimmer and rise –
And the birds are suddenly gone, like children to school,
Vanished into the cool, green depths of the leaves.
A lone egret stalks on the lawn. Nothing else stirs,
Not till the sun, relenting, starts to decline:
Released from fettering heat, out they all fly,
Graceful and airy, flaunting their brilliant hues,
Capricious, agile and jaunty, preening themselves,
Weaving designs on the loom of the late afternoon.

CLOUD PROMISES

We have stopped expecting the rain.
A day has become a burden hard to bear,
Each gritty road a trial to weary feet,
Soil tilled and laboured unrewarding toil,
Crops planted only to wither in the ground.
Thunder's muttering drums are empty boasts,
Repeated promises of rain unkept,
Clouds gather but to drift to another sky,
To water, perhaps, another, greener land.
Our trees are powdered grey with choking dust,
Grown old in a fruitless wait for cleansing rain –
Rain hungered and thirsted for,
By the dry grass, the parched roots,
Rain looked for and longed for,
Rain, take back your pledge, don't trouble yourself –
We have stopped believing in rain.

And then – if then – this week, next week – it rains.

FIRST RAIN

And then at last, at endless last, it rains –
Rain long expected, welcomed back with smiles,
Unfaithful lover returned, all the delays
And broken promises forgiven now –
We kick off shoes to splash on puddled paths
Without reproach, with thankful, outstretched hands,
Singing and dancing in the pouring rain.
The grass grows green again before our eyes,
Wet soil smells rich, the shrubs are hung with gems,

Deep-bedded, silent roots quench endless thirsts,
And half a million birds in every tree,
Their clear notes ringing in the rain-washed air,
Begin to practise songs for wedding days.

RAIN IN TOWN

A hint of moisture in the freshening breeze –
Rain, unmistakable rain, in great scattered drops,
Then a soaring lift of the heart as the heavy clouds burst,
And rain like cavalry thunders across the roof
Towards the open-armed, the exultant trees.
Life-giving rain, cascading out of the skies,
Sweeping headlong and cheerful down rubbish-clogged
drains,
Spouting and gurgling through gutters, gushing wide arcs
From gables and porches and pipes and the holes in old
dustbins,
Playing its sweet water-music in puddles and pools,
Loudly and skilfully drumming on street signs and cars,
On bus shelters, buildings and bicycles, lumbering trucks,
On hats and umbrellas and plastic bags held over heads . . .
Meanwhile, out of sight, screened by sheets of white water,
High branches, light in their ecstasy, frolic and dance with
the rain.

DROWNING WORLD

In former times rain never fell like this,
Washing soil from plants and plants from soil –
Rain fell, enough for harvest, and then ceased.
But now the world is drowning deep and deep,
Gasping, bewildered, overwhelmed, submerged,
Drowning in blinding rain and muddy waters.
Wherever is our wise old rainmaker?
Perhaps he travelled over the hills, away –
And certainly the flooded world will drown.
Perhaps his young boy, tempted by the gifts,
Called up more clouds than he can hold in check,
Keeps trying desperately to stop the rain,
But all in vain, and he and we must drown.
Never again a dry, a sunlit day,
Never the burning sun in a cloudless sky –
Water will pour from the dark grey cloud forever,
And we, the beasts, the crops and the world, will
                                        drown.
Or else, perhaps, the boy is absent-minded,
Idly muses, watches the falling rain –
No hope for us while he thinks of his sweetheart,
Her shyly smiling eyes and dancing feet,
Forgetting the words of power, dreaming his dreams –
And the rain like spears will fall and fall forever,
The rainmaker return to find us drowned.

OCEAN BEACH

Sharp as a knife, honed on the bone-white sand,
Light strikes fierce and bright at sundazzled eyes.
Palm trees quiver with heat, cast trembling shadows,
Surging Atlantic rollers tower and sway,
Break – and pull strongly back, blue under blue sky,
A muffled thunder of drums soothing the shore,
Whispering with foam. A swaggering wind
Patrols the sun-scoured, parched and empty miles.
A little inland, the length of the endless coast,
Unbroken cloud hangs, masking another world,
Sultry, mysterious under the sullen veil.

COASTAL SWAMP

Meandering uncharted channels, swamped by long rains,
Khaki-brown waters lap at the khaki-green trees,
Unmapped acres of mangrove, tenacious, austere:
Two armies contesting the borders of water and land,
Further than eye sees or kites spread their circling flight,
Withdrawing, advancing, outflanking, as patient as Time.
Wearily winding through tangles of strangling bush,
Waterways twist, double, turn, try a thousand paths to the sea,
To its saltwater welcome, fish harvest, its sparkling deeps.
Mangroves, fruitless and obstinate, reach up for light,
Stretch out territorial roots. Bright birds twitter and fly,
And canoes ply steadily, neutrally, under the leaves.

DROUGHT

The merciless sun springs up early to harry the earth,
Blazing with ungoverned anger, aflame with sheer rage,
To bake the dry soil into ashes, to shrivel the trees,
Diminish proud rivers to crawling threads in the sand,
Scorching, unchallenged, whatever catches that eye,
Scorning the measure of months, the bounds of the seasons,
Patient beasts dying for water, pathetic open-beaked birds.
Deaf to appeals for compassion, drunk with its power,
The sun, the implacable sun, beating still harder,
Destroying all that is tender and fragile and green ,
Drinking all moisture, blasting all vigour and joy,
Sparking cruel fire in the forest, cracking the rocks,
Daily delays in its setting, grudging the respite of night.

BEACH WITH FIGURES

Palm trees dance in lines along the beach,
Tossing green heads, shaking wind-blown hair,
Supple and strong, facing the dancing sea.
Austere, brown, comfortless, thatched cabins wait
Silent and empty, swept clean of the sand –
Or blossom, each an exotic fantasy
Splashed with bright cushions, coloured tablecloths,
Alive with talk and laughter, a guitar,
Scented with coffee, sun cream, charcoal smoke –
For a few hours. Then peace. Engines recede,
Racing past wrecks and sandbanks down the creek.
The sea, abandoned playmate, unperturbed,
Withdraws, advances, sways like the dancing trees,
Beguiling, dangerous: and bides its time.

COTTONFIELDS

Cottonfields ready for harvest shimmer in haze –
gardens of roses, rooted in blistering sand,
green and white, fresh and delightful, soothing the eye,
a mirage of coolness. All the while, skin-searing heat
belabours the shoulders, the head, strikes up through shoe
                                                    leather.
Figures austere as the landscape, pared to the bone,
by back-breaking labour as ruthless, as mindless of time,
as stony, implacable, heedless of pain as itself,
wage wars of attrition on scorched earth, force it to flower
with precious, life-giving water prodigally spent –
The desert is blossoming only in bitter defeat.

LIZARD

Full length on the stone-paved terrace lounges the lizard
in navy-blue wetsuit, quite at his arrogant ease,
limbs sprawled in the sun after numberless, effortless
                                                    press-ups.
His age is hard to assess. Not very young. But not old.
That lack-lustre, cynical eye is as sharp as a needle,
on the lookout for females or food or a bit of a barney,
the close-fitting outfit made stylish with orange and grey.
With contemptuous, casual ease he kills a mosquito,
tweaks off bright blossoms to chew from a plant at his elbow.
No companion, no book, no music, no paper. He lounges,
completely engrossed in the business of pleasing himself.

MIGRATING SWALLOWS

The only kind of freedom, open sky:
Our birds-eye lenses sweep the open view
Of changing light and colour, earth and sea,
Unlimited by grudging window frames –
We swing at speed, free, in our element,
Free as the swinging air that carries us
Through the bright day, across the turning world
From home in Europe home to Africa.
Swooping and diving, playing with the wind,
Skimming wide waters south towards the sun,
Over the red-gold, grey-brown desert sand,
The folded ridges, milk-white salty wastes,
The rippling grasslands, nomad cattle herds,
The baked clay cities, friendly sunlit palms.
We ride the smoky haze above thatched roofs,
Catching the dancing midges on the wing,
Headlong and happy. On we race, on and on,
To forest trees in countless shades of green,
Crowding each other, spreading mile on mile,
A vast exuberance of shifting leaves,
Of different scents and blossoms, calls and cries,
Unearthly paradise of heat, flies, rain.

RIVER

The river, glinting silver, gleaming bronze,
Paints its own portrait on the vast green landscape,
Beautifully confident and strong –
Great sweeping loops and smoothly rounded bends
Wind sinuously on and out of sight,
A rhythmic mastery of curve and flow.
Teeming with fish and birds and butterflies,
Collecting tribute as it moves along,
It marries a river of its own degree,
Mirrors a quarter-continent of sky.
Hunting-ground, highway, market, meeting place,
It shares its pride and wealth with river folk
And rules, unchallenged, all its wide domain.
Unwilling to pour its splendid life away,
Watched by the world, into the thirsting seas,
It hesitates, still full of joy and power –
Then, cunning, temporises with its fate,
Delays, dissembles, sends a million streams
Carrying messages and promises
Through the defending walls of mangrove swamps –
Stubbornly stands its ground and will not die.

EARLY EVENING

Streetwise and businesslike, proffering, pleading, cajoling,
Hawkers and beggars with various wares, disabilities,
Blessings and newspapers, roam through the slow-moving traffic.
Passenger-heavy, exhausted, the buses grumble and jostle.
Blue shadows, darker blue, indigo shadows
Soften the fierce light, blunt the sharp edge of the heat.
A thousand and four eager windows won't wait for the darkness
To mirror themselves in the water; unseen, the strong tide
Forges its way through the bridges, the harbour and out to the
                                                    sea.
Headlamps sweep cheerfully homeward to family and food,
Backs turned on emptying offices, shirt collars loosened.

> Hot music spills from the doorways,
> Cooling drinks splash into glasses,
> The tempo is changing, day fading –
> The evening comes into its own.

BEFORE SUNSET

> Tiring at last, the autocratic sun
> Slides out of sight to cool in ocean waters,
> Leaving a silken robe of golden light
> Draped over house fronts and the grateful trees.
> Shadows grow long, incline towards twilight,
> Dragonflies dance their heedless sarabandes,
> Hibiscus bushes burn their blazing lamps,
> And, elegant in their contrasting flight,
> Sunlit and shadowed, low along the creek,
> Fly homeward-going folded paper birds.

VILLAGE DUSK

Sweet woodsmoke drifts through gathering twilight
As cumbersome branches flower into bright fires.
Clay pots, carefully made, gracefully carried
On high heads, strong necks, steadied by capable hands,
Yield up water for washing, for drinking, for cooking.
Children squabble and tumble, teasing and crying,
Are scolded and comforted. Voices grumble and laugh.
Unheeded, the bats circle and dip by the roof thatch
On rapid, swooping manoeuvres, pale in the dusk.
Pestles thump mortars, wielded by vigorous arms;
Those steady, motherly heartbeats, pounding and sounding,
Drum ancient messages, summoning wanderers home.

BALCONY SCENE

Welcoming cushions and a waiting book,
Thin yellow moons of lemon on a dish
And salted peanuts in a wooden bowl –
Release from tensions and the dust of day;
Time to savour sharpening appetite,
Familiar music, friendly silences,
Soft sounds of kitchen promises, faint scents,
Doors set wide open to the balmy dark,
The water rippling, full of tumbled stars.

HIGH LIFE

Music to set deaf men dancing in neighbouring kitchens,
to snare the bright moon in the palm fronds, to hold back the tide.
Passersby jig in the road to the pulsating rhythm,
tailors and traders and secretaries, newspaper boys.
Stewards go hurrying, ice-cubes and glasses a-jingle,
on errands of mercy, attending extravagant thirsts,
or conspiring to break the hospitable back of the table
with well-chosen offerings, spiced to bring tears to the eyes.
Richly embroidered caps, guinea brocades fit for Paradise,
acres of white lace, of opulent hand-woven cloth;
head-ties, silk flights of birds, delicate clustering butterflies,
glittering , rainbow-hued, gorgeous as Solomon's wives –
laughing, surrender themselves to the music's insistence,
spinning in time with each other, the shadows, the stars.

MELLOW MOON

For you I will sing to the resonant drum,
Mellow moon, gracious and yellow,
The spacious midnight sky's familiar guest,
Warm and enormous, scattering greetings and moonbeams,
Smiling on madmen and lovers, dissolving the dark,
Indulging the children clinging to folds of your cloak –
Mellow, round, African moon, warmly yellow,
For you I will weave my tune with the flute and the drum.

NIGHT MARKET

Sunset fades. A pause. The darkness falls,
Complete, warm, velvet-black – no stars, no moon –
Till countless little yellow dancing flames
Spring up on oil-soaked wicks, trail sooty smoke.
Pretty, capricious, fluttering like moths,
Lamps perch by tiny heaps of spices, dyes,
Fitfully shine on lemons, okro, yams,
On alert, watchful eyes of market women,
On upturned faces, sudden brilliant smiles,
A patterned wrapper and a polished arm.
On patient backs, the babies' turning heads,
Sleepily fascinated, safely kept.
Made not ten yards away on busy looms
In a bright daytime world, handwoven cloths
Lie dormant, glimmering with silver threads
Showing a hint of blue, a glint of green.
Beads, buttons, rice, cassava, cowrie shells,
Are vaguely visible in monochrome,
Drained of their colours – but, in fiery pride,
Red peppers blaze, amazingly undimmed,
Superbly scarlet, scorching the mouth of night.

DARKNESS

Darkness sweeps in, overshadows, means to stay,
Heavily settles on the stool of power,
A presence to reckon with, arrogant and old,
Alertly listening to the trembling world –
Black desert, grassland, swamp, black rolling hills,
Black against blackness, painfully awake.
Wide robes waft night-time odours, a humid heat:
Black rivers pulse, dark arteries of dark night:
Black creatures prick their ears, dark forces stir.
Darkness decrees no mercy to be shown:
All homely daytime shapes are wiped away,
Expunged. Primeval bush moves back
Close to the shuttered windows in a bound,
Faithful familiar at the heels of the dark.

DANCING

You should hear us laugh! You should hear us sing!
And oh! - and oh! - but oh! you should see us dance!
We dance in the womb to the beat of the heart,
And are brought forth dancing with cries of surprise
To dance on our sisters' sinuous backs,
On the way to the stream or the market-place.
We dance to the tap of a hammer, a spoon,
To the slapping of paddles or rain on the thatch.
In sadness or anger, hunger or joy,
We dance – for a wedding, for the pleasure of life,

For a chief at a feast, for a close friend dead;
For a traveller returned, for a child newborn,
For no good reason, or in God's good praise.
As our eyes grow dim, in sorrow and pain,
Though our bodies grow old, we go dancing on
To the pulsing beat of the tireless drums,
With our children's children, their neighbours and wives,
Without even stopping for our burial day –
Till at length our steps make no pattern of sound,
Not a rustle, not a whisper in the listening wind,
And we fade like shadows on our noiseless feet –
And all that is left
                        is a memory
                                    dancing.

POETIC LICENCE

BLACK AND WHITE BLUES

A place in the shade and a truly sensational view:
Time to unwind, find a melody flowing and true,
But without pen and paper to hand, what's a poet to do?
Sunk deep in gloom with no-one but myself to accuse
I've got a bad case of the No Pen, No Paper Blues.

The hills and the sky and the sea please the eye,
And then random words tease, until honed and refined
Into phrases conveying the scene to the mind,
Just as vividly clear but now pleasing the ear –
But, a fool without tools and a prey to regret,
Like a fisherman parted from rod, line and net,
I sit here bemoaning rare moments too precious to lose,
Dolefully singing the No Pen, No Paper Blues.

My restless hand itches for implements known or unknown,
To be happily scratching in wax with a fragment of bone
Or chipping with hammer and chisel at tablets of stone.
Pokerwork? Parchment? Papyrus? The West Sussex News?
Nothing there but despair and the No Pen, No Paper Blues.

A butterfly thought demands to be caught
In sharp black on white, a delight to the sight
In its pattern and elegant , wandering flight:
But I can't even think without pen and ink,
Can't savour the flavour of rhythm and rhyme
Nor snatch at the forelock of ticktocking Time.
What offering is it to proffer a visiting Muse
In wailing frustration, my No Pen, No Paper Blues?

I'll order a fourth cup of coffee, though I've drunk my fill:
I see napkins from here in a pile by the side of the till
So while you are there, will you spare me a few with my bill?
And lend me your pencil, please, waiter, oh, do not refuse,
I'm feeling so low with the No Pen, No Paper Blues.

TIME IS NOT OLD

Time is not old, quite the opposite. Young and untamed,
Time is impetuous, self-willed and knows no restraint.
An uncontrolled force, an earthquake, a landslide, a hurricane,
It ruthlessly brushes aside as unwanted rubbish
Irreplaceable treasures amassed over lifetimes.
Time rewrites the history books, alters mathematics and grammar,
The accepted meaning of words and the rules of lawn tennis.
It changes the streets and the squares of the cities you love
Until you may well lose your way round the palm of your hand.
Lord of misrule, Time gives rein to the actions of upstarts,
Of vandals, invaders, insurgents and government men.
It swaggers about, flaunting some freakish new fashion,
Wearing holes in new carpets, old flagstones, the atmosphere, even,
And favours the brash ignoramus. It cuts down the trees
And sweeps away temples. It mocks at the wisdom of ages.
Time has no time for experience. Time is not old.

SECOND OPINION:

Time simply is! It cannot be old, young or dated.
It is there: to be harnessed, like gravity, water or fire,
Or wasted, like money, or warm summer days, moonlit nights.
Perhaps you don't get out enough? The opera, ballet,
Or a weekend down in the country, once in a while?
We must not be betrayed into hurling abuse at the calendar,
Taking issue with yardsticks. Rod, pole or perch,
Time is a measure, usefully marked off in sections.
A little more of whatever you fancy cuts Time down to size –
And Time, like the tides, can wash unearned delights to your feet.

POETIC PRIVILEGE

Rhyme is an option, neither cage nor chain.
Our treasure-store of language, rich with choice,
Proffers a wide variety of forms
Each offering the voice, in different keys,
The means to make a music all its own.
Ranging through many a change in tone and pace,
Perhaps words may seem flung with careless ease,
Free to fall at random; by happy chance –
Or subtle skill – they dance across the page,
Sob out their grief, rage bitter fury – or
Record quiet conversations with a friend.
To please the seeing eye, the attentive ear,
Not every poem reaches for a rhyme.

Song For Don Giovanni

O turn your lovely head
And let me see your face;
Along the path you tread
You move with grace.

Before you speak a word
I know your voice is sweet –
Sweeter than singing bird
In summer heat.

My heart can wear no disguise;
I give you my nights and days
Now that you lift your eyes
And meet my gaze.

Nothing can be the same
Ever on earth or sea;
Forget your home, your name.
And stay with me.

TROUBADOUR'S SONG

O listen to my song;
Turn that sweet face to me.
The heart that was my own
Does now to you belong
And yours must ever be.
I sing for you alone
Of all my joy and pain,
Not fearing cold disdain –
Your heart is not of stone.

Those clear eyes and kind,
Filled with a modest grace,
Can find for false pride no room,
But are windows on a mind
As lovely as your face,
The garden's sweetest bloom.
My song is the breeze that blows
Softly over that rose,
Borrowing its perfume.

Wherever my song is sung
Will be, all thanks to you,
More fragrant than before;
With your praises on my tongue,
Wherever the breeze blows through
Spilling its precious store,
I shall be transported here,
You will be forever near,
Even on the most distant shore.

POETIC LICENCE

When all is said and done,
This wide world is our heritage;
Though there's nothing new under the sun,
We've fresh words for every page.

So, no lines of orange cones
Guarding daffodils in Spring;
No wide exclusion zones
If nightingales should sing.

No order to desist
From tiger or lamb or lark,
Or rainbow or autumn mist –
Fair's fair, it's hands off the Snark.

No copyright applied
To all the winds that blow;
No right of way denied
Past woodland in the snow.

No veto on lizard or snake,
A red rose, or the light of the moon;
No embargo on hearts that break,
Or on darkness that falls too soon.

No shouting of vulgar abuse
If we mention a cherry tree;
No bar on unlimited use
Of ships and the call of the sea.

No prohibition shrill –
There's no such word as don't –
If we choose to rhyme we will,
And otherwise we won't.

While the earth still circles the sun
And the stars have yet to fall,
All is not said and done
And painted once and for all.

IN PRAISE OF DOGGEREL

A poem, to be a real poem,
In my book, at least, has to rhyme;
All that blank verse and high-minded rubbish
Is simply a sad waste of time.

What I need is my kind of poet,
Not these superior blokes
Who write to impress one another,
With no rhyme or reason or jokes.

Good poets express themselves clearly,
With passion, precision and pith –
Yes – but using everyday language
As if they were our kin and kith.

I like that kind of poem,
Not a lot of strange words on a string;
Something light-hearted and catchy,
That goes with a bit of a swing.

So come on, now! Sharpen your pencil
And knock out a poem today –
But please don't expect any payment –
You ought to know Rhyme doesn't Pay.

Postcard from home

I picked up the post and twirled into a dance –
I know your handwriting at first glance,
And before I have read what you have to say,
A letter from you is a sunny day.

UNBROKEN PROMISES

Later the day will be hot. Now the chill morning river
Runs its cold fingers along the trailed hems of the gardens,
Gurgling and chuckling, tugging at grasses and buttercups.
Reflections of intricate brickwork, ruffled and rippling,
In tawny-rose, yellow and crimson, all shot through with silver,
Form a cloak of brilliant feathers stirred by the breeze.
Seen from the water, the dark mirrored arches of bridges
Create a wavering tunnel, inviting, unreal,
Leading upstream and rich in unbroken promises.
I have been that way many times, in a long-ago boat,
Pulling against the strong current, out into thin mists
And beyond, to where swans dip quiet heads, where fish glide
                                                    and swirl,
Where unseen birds scatter the raindrops from sheltering trees;
At length to return - an effortless ride past green meadows
On the sinewy back of the vigorous, fast-flowing river,
Unperturbed by my stowaway boat or the sound of my singing.

FLIGHTS OF FANCY

A perfect summer morning,
Full of birds and butterflies;
To be walking past the hangars
I need only close my eyes.

A chat with the mechanic –
Friends wave to us as they pass –
Magneto fixed – a tyre changed –
Smell of oil and fresh cut grass.

My Avro-Anson's ready,
Routine checks all carefully done;
Time to talk to the control tower
Now I've let my engines run.

A strong breeze from the south-west,
And Met Office says no rain;
Earth drops away, air takes our weight,
And we climb the skies again.

Not every man is given
The job he loves the best;
Caution mixed with danger
Gives mine its special zest.

A slight easing of the throttle
To tune the engine's song,
Fields and toy houses far below:
Here I am, where I belong.

THE KITE

My heart, flying high, is a kite,
With you the air under my wings;
If it seems I shall soar out of sight,
       You are the strings.

You are the sun on my face,
Unless it burns too fierce and proud;
Then, to temper the heat, in its place
       You are the cloud.

You are the lands far below,
You are the castles in Spain;
When the parched desert winds blow,
       You are the rain.

You are the rose and the ring,
You are the face in the throng;
You are the first breath of Spring,
       And the words of my song.

BLANK PAGE BLUES

I've got the right kind of paper and my favourite pen –
No window-cleaners, no delivery men.
I've got the right sort of table at the right sort of height,
A good working atmosphere, and good natural light;
A comfortable chair, neither soft nor hard,
And neatly written notes on a plain white card –
But to my consternation, not a hint of inspiration.
I've got the What's Happened to my Muse? Blues.

I had a healthy breakfast but I didn't overdo it;
(I eyed a second croissant but thought later I might rue it)
I've already done the crossword and the daily isn't due,
I've paid the wretched gas bill, and the wretched plumber, too.
My mind is on my writing and the blank page is inviting –
But, imagine my vexation, not a jot of inspiration,
Only the What's Happened to my Muse? Blues.

The telephone is silent and nobody knows I'm in;
There's coffee at my elbow, next to biscuits in a tin.
My thoughts are clear, my will-power will not waver –
But it seems as if the salt has lost its savour.
My mood is calm and steady and my brain is at the ready
For the job I have to finish; but my certainties diminish.
Have you any helpful views? Or a really cunning ruse?
What detail can be lacking? Must I clothe myself in sacking?
Nothing comes. No inspiration. Only howling desolation
And the Whatever Can Have Happened to my Muse? Blues.

GLAD TO BE ME

ALL THE ROADS LEAD TO RUDGWICK

All the roads lead to Rudgwick,
Each morning, with no end of bustle and clamour,
From Gatwick and Guildford and Abinger Hammer.
Rudgwick's a specially interesting spot –
Just follow the road, you will like it a lot.

All the roads lead to Rudgwick.
From Horsham or Loxwood just hop on the bus:
If you can't believe it, ask any of us.
Rudgwick is brilliant, Rudgwick is neat –
You can ask anyone down our street.

All the roads lead to Rudgwick,
From Billingshurst, Warnham and Wisborough Green,
And hundreds of villages in between,
Because Rudgwick's a magnet and Rudgwick is cool –
You can ask anyone at our school:
All the roads lead to Rudgwick!

THE FLYING BANANA

He bought a yellow bicycle
From someone saving for a cello;
New brakes, new saddle, and a tin of paint
To paint it a better shade of yellow.

APPLE TREE ALLEY

When my favourite shoes tap out intricate patterns
All the way along Cherry Tree Street,
People come running to open their windows,
Watching me merrily marking the beat.

People come running out of their houses
To try out new dance steps all down the hill,
But I am swept off on a floodtide of music,
Footing it featly with cunning and skill.

Drumming and thrumming, a light-hearted rhythm
Is sounding right through me, witty and sweet,
Dot-and-carrying syncopation
Straight to my happily pattering feet.

Twirling and whirling past Peach Tree Terrace,
Through Plum Tree Crescent and on past the shops,
I skip and I trip into Apple Tree Alley,
Where the music slows: and, then . . . finally . . . stops.

A PRIVATE PLACE

You know you have a special, private place
That you can visit, kept inside your head?
I expect you'd like to tell me all about it,
But I'm going to tell you all about mine instead.

Nobody can come unless I ask them;
No one stays if I send them away.
I make the rules, and, if I choose, I change them,
And everyone does exactly what I say.

Just now it's rather full of fairy fashions,
With lots of sparkly clothes in purple and pink;

My favourite characters are all invited –
We'll have a fancy-dress parade, I think.

Next week I could be living in the mountains,
Or roller-blading in a circus act;
I never fall, no matter what I'm doing –
I'm amazing! I'm the heroine, in fact.

I can ride a one-wheel cycle with my eyes shut;
Cook delicious meals; break open castle doors.
I'm so happy in my lovely, magic country,
There's no time for me to come and visit yours.

BROOMSTICK POEM

You probably know I can fly.
We take off, my sister and I,
Go twice round the room, quick,
Each guiding her broomstick,
Then off we zoom, into the sky.

Rudgwick looks great from up there,
And a cooling breeze blows through our hair;
Over Pennthorpe we swoop,
Neatly looping the loop,
And up past the church to the fair.

It's quite easy, once you begin;
Keep your head up, and both elbows in.
We both got so canny
By learning with Granny –
But she can fly backwards and spin.

WILFRED & ALFRED

Alfred lives in the world in the mirror
And he's friendly and ready to play;
His hair grows exactly as mine does,
And is brushed at the same time of day.

He laughs when I'm laughing and happy;
He's pleased to see I'm feeling fine;
He can pull some really weird faces –
And he does when I'm practising mine.

My name's Wilfred and his name is Alfred;
I've known him always and a week –
And if we climbed through to each other,
We'd be able to hear ourselves speak.

GLAD TO BE ME

I like to play princesses
But I'm glad I'm really me;
They never went on holiday
Or had a friend to tea.

I'm glad I'm not Rapunzel
With all that hair to dry,
Or poor little Cinderella,
Left alone to cry.

They never went out shopping
Or learnt to swim or ski.
I like to play princesses
But I'm glad I'm really me.

SU DOKU POEM

Doing Su Doku is fun,
You don't have to be a great brain;
Know your numbers, starting with one
Up to nine, and then back down again.

The first few answers, you'll find,
Are amazingly easy to fit;
The next can be more of a grind,
But the end is the easiest bit.

Before you have even begun,
I'm quite sure that you are aware
Nine squares nine times make eighty one –
And they all fit inside one big square.

If I'm waiting to get on a plane
It is entertaining to do,
Or if rattling along on a train –
But it's most fun if I am with you.

THE RUNAWAY

He pedalled away in his new toy car,
Right past the church at the end of the street,
A long way at his age – but not as far
As he might have gone on his own two feet.

He was hot and tired and lonely and sad,
Wishing he'd never decided to roam,
When, just at that moment, his best friend's dad
Gave him an ice-cream and helped him home.

KEYS

Selecting a heavy book, down on my knees,
I saw my forgotten collection of keys
And tipped them all out, to admire them again
Like some miser. So many! Embellished and plain,
Iron, brass, silver or steel. Finely wrought,
Old, friendly, unmatching; some found and some bought.
This one was given. This was used as a weight
On Grandfather's papers. This one is not straight.
So many secrets are waiting for me –
Somewhere a lock to fit every key!
A deed-box, a priest's hole, a highwayman's lair;
A cupboard concealing a dark, winding stair;
A great treasure-chest; a green garden door;
A gate to the steep path down to the shore;
An old suitcase – a cottage – an ivory box . . .
Do my keys, lying dormant, remember their locks?
I shall sort them and label them just as I please,
Then put them all back in their own box, marked KEYS.

PAVLOV'S DUCKS

You can't really call them wild mallard –
They have lost any right to the name;
Once they tasted the grain scattered for them,
They lost self-respect and all shame.

They spend all day looking for handouts –
What impudent beggars they are!
They rush off to pester the postman
Or anyone coming by car.

I'm tired of this hustling and quacking;
I'm starting to feel put upon;
It was all very well in the winter,
But winter's long over and gone.

They are almost too portly for takeoff,
The victims of gross appetite;
Their feathers are glossy and gleaming,
Their greedy eyes watchful and bright.

And the lake is seething with ducklings –
Their unions are still bearing fruit.
It was highest quality bird-seed –
And so highly addictive to boot.

PUMA

'There's a puma in the paddock!' said young Edward.
'A puma jumped the fence, he's in the thistles!
Is it alright if I shoot it? There's a pheasant
All gold and red and sweeping summer feathers,
And magpies skimming off other business,
And not a single rabbit out this morning.
But this puma met my eye as if it knew me,
And crouched, and lashed its tail a bit, and waited
And watched me as I came to ask about it.
Might it perhaps belong to some old neighbour?
I don't want to annoy it, like the postman,
But it doesn't seem right just to take no notice.
So what do you think? What's the rule for pumas?'

SECRET PACT

'I like the cut of your jib, your style',
Said the smiling moon to me;
Then he glided behind some chimney pots
And untangled himself from a tree.

'I saw you all in the back of the car,
Like puppies curled up in a heap,
And I couldn't help wondering who you are,
The only one not asleep.'

He slid over some roofs for the fun of it
And took a short cut at a bend:
'So I thought I would follow along for a bit
And ask you to be my friend.'

It all seemed stranger than strange to me –
What could it be about?
I was only one of a family
And not usually singled out.

Perhaps a mistake? Or a teasing joke?
I could find nothing to say,
But though I smiled shyly and never spoke,
The moon followed all the way.

And now, on any calm, moonlit night,
By the sea – on a hill – in the street –
Moonbeams reach out to me, cool and bright,
Wherever, whenever we meet.

GREEN FINGERS

Never grown a carrot-top or any flower at all from seed?
We're very near the flower shop – it's an amaryllis bulb you need.
Pot it by the kitchen sink in the compost they provide,
And in fewer days than you would think –

                        green leaves spring tall and wide.
Once started, it grows beanstalk quick, at an angle, near the edge.
(Unless you prop it with a stick it will topple off the window ledge.)
Add some water, and any day you'll see a stem reach for the moon
And swell to a bud. Don't go away – the crowning moment is

                                coming soon:
As if to a silent trumpet-call, gorgeous flowers burst their way out –
And a second stem forms last of all, for a final triumphant victory

                                      shout.

IN OTHER WORDS

Poems translated by the author

DENKEND Aan HOLLAND

Denkend aan Holland zie ik brede rivieren
Traag door oneindig laagland gaan,
Rijen ondenkbaar ijle populieren
Als hoge pluimen aan den einder staan:
En in de geweldige ruimte verzonken
De boerderijen verspreid door het land,
Boemgroepen, dorpen, geknotte torens
Kerken en olmen in een groots verband.
De lucht hangt er laag en de zon wordt er langzaam
In grijze veelkleurige dampen gesmoord,
En in alle gewesten wordt de stem van het water
Met zijn eeuwige rampen gevreesd en gehoord.

H.Marsman (1899 - 1940)

THINKING OF HOLLAND

To think of Holland is for me to see
wide rivers through endless lowlands dawdling go;
at the horizon, poplars like tall plumes
inconceivably slender, stand in row;
and scattered all across the landscape, farms
sunk in a spaciousness that overwhelms
in a great network linked to villages,
copses and flat-topped towers, churches and elms.
There the sky hangs low and there the sun
in grey multicoloured mists is slowly drowned,
and the voice of water, calamitous forever,
is feared and heard in all the country round.

LES HIBOUX

Sous les ifs noirs qui les abritent,
Les hiboux se tiennent rangés,
Ainsi que des dieux étrangers,
Dardant leur oeil rouge. Ils méditent.

Sans remuer ils se tiendront
Jusqu'à l'heure mélancholique
Ou, poussant le soleil oblique,
Les ténèbres s'établiront.

Leur attitude au sage enseigne
Qu'il faut en ce monde qu'il craigne
Le tumulte et le mouvement ;

L'homme ivre d'une ombre qui passe
Porte toujours le châtiment
D'avoir voulu changer de place.

Charles Baudelaire (1821 - 1867)

THE OWLS

Under black yews they sit and wait,
Owls like alien deities,
Eyes darting red fire from the sheltering trees,
All in a line. They meditate.

Quite immobile they will stay
Until that melancholy hour
When darkness comes to impose its power,
Thrusting the slanting sun away.

The wise man, studying their poise,
Learns movement and excessive noise
Are not the habits to embrace.

The man by passing whims beguiled
Is dealt with like a naughty child
For aspiring to a change of place.

PENDANT LA TEMPÊTE

La barque est petite et la mer immense
La vague nous jette au ciel en courroux,
Le ciel nous renvoie au flot en démence :
Près du mât rompu prions à genoux !

De nous à la tombe il n'est qu'une planche :
Peut-être ce soir, dans un lit amer,
Sous un froid linceul, fait d'écume blanche,
Irons nous dormir, veillés par l'éclair.

Fleur du paradis, sainte Notre-Dame,
Si bonne aux marins en péril de mort,
Apaise le vent, fais taire la lame,
Et pousse du doigt notre esquif au port.

Nous te donnerons, si tu nous délivres,
Une belle robe en papier d'argent,
Un cierge à festons pesant quatre livres,
Et, pour ton Jésus, un petit Saint-Jean.

Théophile Gautier (1811 - 1872)

STORM AT SEA

The waves hurl us up to the angry sky –
Our boat is little, the sea is vast –
The sky flings us back to mad breakers high,
And we fall to our knees by the broken mast.

There is only a plank between us and doom;
Maybe tonight in a cheerless bed
We shall sleep, coldly shrouded in white sea-spume,
With lightning flickering overhead.

Holy Mary, Flower of Heaven, kind
To sailors in peril on the sea,
Still the billows and calm the wind
Guide us to the haven where we would be.

We will bring, if you save us in our distress,
A great, heavy candle, and to put on
A beautiful silver-paper dress –
And, for your Jesus, a little Saint John.

NOËL

Le ciel est noir, la terre est blanche ;
Cloches, carillonez gaîment !
Jésus est né; la Vierge penche
Sur lui son visage charmant.

Pas de courtines festonnées
Pour préserver l'enfant du froid ;
Rien que des toiles d'araignées
Qui pendent des poutres du toit.

Il tremble sur la paille fraîche
Ce cher petit enfant Jésus
Et pour l'échauffer dans sa crèche
L'âne et le boeuf soufflent dessus.

La neige du chaume pend ses franges
Mais sur le toit s'ouvre le ciel
Et, tout en blanc, le choeur des anges
Chante aux bergers: 'Noël ! Noël !'

Théophile Gautier (1811 - 1872)

CHRISTMAS

The sky is black, the earth is white;
Ring out, bells, peals of joy!
Jesus is born; and, charming sight,
The Virgin leans close to her little boy.

No ornate curtains around his bed
Protect the infant from the cold;
Spiders drape long webs instead
From the roof-beams, fold on fold.

Dear little baby Jesus now
Lies shivering on the chilly hay
And, with their breath, the ass and cow
Keep him warm as best they may.

Snow hangs from the thatched roof of the byre;
Above, heaven's portals stand ajar
And all in white the angelic choir
Sings to the shepherds: "Gloria!"

PASTEL

J'aime à vous voir en vos cadres ovales
Portraits jaunis des belles du vieux temps,
Tenant en main des roses un peu pâles,
Comme il convient à des fleurs de cent ans.

Le vent d'hiver, en vous touchant la joue,
A fait mourir vos oeillets et vos lis,
Vous n'avez plus que des mouches de boue
Et sur les quais vous gisez tout salis.

Il est passé, le doux règne des belles ;
La Parabère avec la Pompadour
Ne trouveraient que des sujets rebelles,
Et sous leur tombe est enterré l'amour.

Vous, cependent, vieux portraits qu'on oublie,
Vous respirez vos bouquets sans parfums,
Et souriez avec mélancolie
Au souvenir de vos galants défunts.

Théophile Gautier (1811- 1872)

PASTEL

I love to see you in your oval frames,
Hands holding roses now turned somewhat pale,
You faded portraits of old-fashioned dames:
Hundred-year-old flowers must need be frail.

Winter's wind has chilled your cheeks' warm blood –
Carnations, lilies, won't bloom there again;
Your beauty spots are merely flecks of mud;
You lie on grimy quays along the Seine.

The gentle reign of beauties is no more;
Parabère, Pompadour have lost their throne
Never to find the homage of before;
Love's buried under their memorial stone.

Yet, forgotten, in outmoded styles,
Sniffing at your unperfumed nosegays,
Still you smile your melancholy smiles,
Remembering dead loves of former days.

CHINOISERIE

Ce n'est pas vous, non, madame, que j'aime
Ni vous non plus, Juliette, ni vous,
Ophélie ni Béatrice, ni même
Laure la blonde, avec ses grands yeux doux.

Celle que j'aime, à présent, est en Chine;
Elle demeure avec ses vieux parents
Dans une tour de porcelaine fine,
Au fleuve Jaune, ou sont les cormorans.

Elle a des yeux retroussés vers les tempes,
Un pied petit à tenir dans la main,
Le teint plus clair que le cuivre des lampes,
Les ongles longs et rougis de carmin.

Par son treillis elle passe sa tête,
Que l'hirondelle en volant vient toucher ;
Et, chaque soir, autant qu'un poête,
Chante le saule et la fleur du pêcher.

Théophile Gautier (1811 - 1872)

CHINOISERIE

No, Madam, it is not you I adore,
Nor you, Juliet – you're not the one I prize,
Nor Ophelia, nor Beatrice, no more
Than fair haired Laura with her large, sweet eyes.

For now, my love in China does remain,
Dwelling with aged parents, at their wish,
In a tower made of finest porcelain
By the Yellow River, where the cormorants fish.

She has eyes set a-slanting in her head;
Her little foot would fit into my hand;
Her fingernails are long and carmine red,
Her skin more clear than brass lamp on a stand.

She puts her head out from her trellis bower –
The swallow dips to touch it in its flight –
And she sings of willows and the peach in flower,
Like any poet, at the fall of night.

L'INVITATION AU VOYAGE

Mon enfant, ma soeur,
Songe à la douceur
D'aller là-bas vivre ensemble !
Aimer à loisir,
Aimer et mourir
Au pays qui te ressemble !
Les soleils mouillés
De ses ciels brouillés
Pour mon esprit ont les charmes
Si mystérieux
De tes traîtres yeux,
Brillant à travers leurs larmes.

Là, tout n'est qu'ordre et beauté,
Luxe, calme et volupté.

Des meubles luiusants,
Polis par les ans,
Décoreraient notre chambre ;
Les plus rares fleurs
Mêlant leurs odeurs
Aux vagues senteurs de l'ambre ;
Les riches plafonds,
Les miroirs profonds,
La splendeur orientale,
Tout y parlerait
A l'âme en secret
Sa douce langue natale.

Là, tout n'est qu'ordre et beauté,
Luxe, calme et volupté.

Vois, sur ces canaux

Dormir ces vaisseaux

Dont l'humeur est vagabonde ;

C'est pour assouvir

Ton moindre désir

Qu'ils viennent du bout du monde.

– Les soleils couchants

Revêtent les champs,

Les canaux, la ville entière,

D'hyacinthe et d'or ;

Le monde s'endort

Dans une chaude lumière.

Là, tout n'est qu'ordre et beauté,

Luxe, calme et volupté.

Charles Baudelaire (1821 - 1867)

INVITATION TO A VOYAGE

Dream, my sister, my child,

How with pleasure beguiled

We might journey to dwell there, we two;

To love at our ease,

Love until our lives cease,

In the land that reminds me of you.

That moisture-veiled sun

Shares a mystery at one –

So to me it appears –

In its rain-clouded skies,

With your own faithless eyes,

Shining through their tears.

There, all is order and beauty,
Calm, and voluptuous luxury.

Gleaming veneers
Polished by the years
Would ornament our chamber,
The rarest of blooms
Mingling their perfumes
With the faint smell of amber;
Rich ceilings and fine,
Deep mirrors ashine
Eastern splendours among –
Secretly, the whole
Would speak to the soul
Its sweet native tongue.

There, all is order and beauty,
Calm, and voluptuous luxury.

On canals, see, there sleep
Great ships of the deep
Whose nature's to roam;
It is to satisfy
Your caprices they ply
Round the world, far from home.
The setting sun's glow
Canal and meadow
And the whole town is steeping
In topaz, golden-bright;
In the warm blush of light
The world falls asleeping.

There, all is order and beauty,
Calm, and voluptuous luxury.

LA PIPE

Je suis la pipe d'un auteur;
On voit, à contempler ma mine
D'Abyssinienne ou de Cafrine,
Que mon maître est un grand fumeur.

Quand il est comblé de douleur,
Je fume comme la chaumine
Ou se prépare la cuisine
Pour le retour du laboureur.

J'enlace et je berce son âme
Dans le réseau mobile et bleu
Qui monte da ma bouche en feu
Et je roule un puissant dictame
Qui charme son coeur et guérit
De ses fatigues son esprit.

Charles Baudelaire (1821 - 1867)

THE PIPE

I'm an author's pipe; and as you see
From my dark-complexioned face,
As if born in some outlandish place,
My master smokes me constantly.

When cares his spirits overturn
I smoke just like some little cot
Where dinner simmers in the pot
Against the labourer's return.

I enfold his mind and lull it well
In the blue web, drifting higher,
That issues from my mouth of fire;
And I weave a potent spell,
With which his aching heart I bless,
And ease his inner weariness.

LE GUANCE DE LA MIA PASTORELLUCCIA

Le guance de la mia pastorelluccia
Rassembran proprio due mele rosciole;
I gentil labbri de la sua boccuccia
Paron due fraganelle volte al sole,
E le sue carne odoran de mentuccia
E de silvestre e mammole vïole;
Le tette sono dur, vaghette e belle
Che par che sien due mele caponcelle.

Olimpo da Sassoferrato (1486 - 1540)

MY SHEPHERDESS

The cheeks of my buxom shepherdess
Are rosy pippins, ripe each one;
Her sweet and luscious lips, no less
Than strawberries, turned to the sun;
Wild mint and meadow flowers caress
Her body, their fragrance now her own;
Her lovely breasts, firm, unconfined,
Bring two round apples to my mind.

NIENTE DA ASPETTARE

Niente da aspettare
Niente da temere
Niente chiedere – e tutto dare
Non andare
Ma permanere.
Non c'è premio, non c'è posa.
La vita è tutta una dura cosa.

Carlo Michelstaedter (1887 - 1910)

NOTHING TO HOPE FOR

Nothing to hope for
Nothing to dread
Asking for nothing, but instead
Giving everything, nothing gaining,
Never departing, always remaining –
There's no reward, there is no rest.
Life is a bleak affair at best.

VA, PENSIERO

Va', pensiero, sull'ali dorate,
Va, ti posa sui clivi, sui colli,
ove olezzano tepide e molli
l'aure dolci del suolo natal!
Del Giordano le rive saluta,
di Sionne le torri atterrate...
O mia Patria sì bella e perduta!
O membranza sì cara e fatal!
Arpa d'or dei fatidici vati,
perché muta dal salice pendi?
Le memorie nel petto raccendi,
ci favella del tempo che fu!
O simile di Solima ai fati,
traggi un suono di crudo lamento;
o t'ispiri il Signore un concento
che ne infonda al patire virtù!

Chorus of the Hebrew Slaves from *'Nabucco'* by Verdi.
Librettist, Temistocle Solera.

BY THE WATERS OF BABYLON

Come, my thoughts, now on golden wing take flight
To the slopes and hillsides that I used to know;
To my native land go, and there alight
Where gentle, warm, sweet-scented breezes blow!
Greet from me the banks of Jordan river
And the fallen towers of Zion's city:
Lovely homeland, lost to me forever!
Precious memories filled with love and pity!
You golden harp of the prophetic seers,
Why hang there silent in the willow tree?
Revive in us remembrance of past years!
Sing us tales of the days that used to be!
Like Jerusalem, shriek back in Fortune's face,
Or, inspired by the Lord's self, by the Deity,
Sound out a harmony of such grace
It endows our suffering with nobility!

*Translated by the author at the request of an impromptu
choir on a Swan Hellenic cruise.*

VENEZIA

C'é una città di questo mondo,
Ma così bella, ma così strana,
Che pare un gioco di fata morgana
O una visione del cuor profondo.

Avviluppata in uno roseo velo,
Sta con sue chiese palazzi giardini
Tutta sospesa tra due turchini,
Quello del mare, quello del cielo.

Così mutevole! A volte
Nelle mattine di sole bianco,
Splende d'un riso pallido e stanco,
D'un chiuso lume, come la perla;

Ma nei tramonti rossi affocati
È un arca d'oro, ardente, raggianti,
Nave immense veleggiante
A lontani lidi incantati.

Quando la luna alta inargenta
Torri snelle e cupole piene
E serpeggia per cento vene
D'acqua cupa e sonnolenta,

Non si può dire quel ch'ella sia,
Tanto è nuova mirabile cosa:
Isola sacra misteriosa,
Regno infinito di fantasia . . .

Cosa di sogno, vaga e leggera;
Eppure porta mill'anni di storia,
E si corona della gloria
D'una grande vita guerriera.

Diego Valeri (1887 - 1986)

VENICE

A city of this world, yet set apart,
Being so other, and in such beauty decked,
She seems a vision or mirage-effect
Conjured up from deep within the heart.
Swathed in a rose-pink veil, she's floating free
With her churches, gardens, palaces,
Between a pair of matching turquoises,
Between the blue of the sky, the blue of the sea.

So changeable! Perhaps she'll gleam awhile,
Under the white sun of an early day,
With a muted and a pearl-like ray,
Smiling a pallid and exhausted smile.
Yet, when its fiery red the sunset pours,
She flames and sparkles; she's a golden boat,
A mighty vessel, now afloat,
Sailing to distant and enchanted shores.

When the moon drops silver from the height
On to slender towers and rounded domes,
And snaking through the slumbering water, roams
Through a hundred veins as dark as night –
One really cannot say what she may be
In this unheard of and amazing style:
A sacred and mysterious isle,
A boundless realm of fantasy.

As a thing of dreams she may be seen –
Yet, robed in a thousand years of story,
She's wearing as her crown the glory
Of her great life as warrior queen.

ACUARELA

Con el cielo gris
la copla
triste de Sevilla
se afina, se afina.
En agua sin sol
sombras de naranjos
entierran azahares.
Arriba,
En las altas miras
esperan las niñas
los barcos de oro
Abajo
aguardan los mozos
que se abran cancelas
a patios sin fondo.
Sin rubor se quedan,
pálidas, las torres.
Desde las orillas
las desesperadas
luces suicidas
al río se lanzan.
Cadáveres lentos
rosa, verde, azul,
azul, verde, rosa
se los lleva el agua.

Pedro Salinas (1891-1951)

WATERCOLOUR

It is under grey skies
That the sad songs of Seville
Are honed to perfection.

Shadows of orange trees
Bury their blossoms
In sunless waters.

Up yonder, from high vantage points,
Young girls keep their look-out
For gold-laden vessels.

Below, boys watch for gates to be opened
Into deep, endlessly deep
Courtyard gardens.

Towers stand still,
Wan and unblushing.

From the banks
Despairing lights
Fling themselves suicidally
Into the river.

Their slow-moving bodies,
Pink, green, blue,
Blue, green, pink,
Are borne along by the water.

Printed by: Copytech (UK) Limited trading as Printondemand-worldwide,
9 Culley Court, Bakewell Road, Orton Southgate, Peterborough PE2 6XD